The Secret Brain

The Secret Brain

Selected Poems 1995–2012

Dave Brinks

Black Widow Press is an imprint of Commonwealth Books, Inc., Boston, MA. Distributed to the trade by NBN (National Book Network) throughout North America, Canada, and the U.K. All Black Widow Press books are printed on acid-free paper, and glued into bindings. Black Widow Press and its logo are registered trademarks of Commonwealth Books, Inc.

Joseph S. Phillips and Susan J. Wood, Ph.D, Publishers
www.blackwidowpress.com

Book Design: Kerrie Kemperman
Front Cover Design: Dave Brinks
Cover Art: *The Secret Brain* by Dave Brinks
Author Photo: Chris Granger

ISBN-13: 9780985612214

Printed in the United States

10 9 8 7 6 5 4 3 2 1

ACKNOWLEDGEMENTS

The author offers gracious acknowledgement to those publishers and editors who generously featured selections of these works in their publications:

Journals

Anemone, Big City Lit, Brown Box, Constance, Double Dealer Redux, Exquisite Corpse, Fell Swoop, Gathering of the Tribes, Jejune, L – pantheon, La Reata, Lungfull, Meena, Mesechabe, New Delta Review, New Laurel Review, New Orleans Review, Plunge, Rogue Wave, Simpatico, Sinister Goat, Solid Quarter, Steaua, The Tsatsawassans, Trope 5, Unmoveable Feast, Xavier Review, XConnect, YAWP: a Journal of Poetry & Art

Magazines

ArtVoices, Gambit Weekly, Louisiana Cultural Vistas, Scrisul Românesc (Romania), *Sound of Wind, New American Voices* (Albania), *Shambhala Sun, The Nation, VLAK* (Czech Republic)

Anthologies

Another South, Big Bridge, Exquisite Corpse Annual, From a Bend in the River, Holy Tomato, I Was Indian, Maple Leaf Rag III, Maple Leaf Rag IV, Thus Spake the Corpse, What Can't Be Lost: 88 Stories and Traditions from the Sacred City

"Going Back to Water" was originally published in a small edition of hand-made books by Simpatico Press in 2006.

"Concerto in Nine Fragments, Andante" was originally published in a small edition of hand-made books by Simpatico Press in 2007.

"The Tree House Aquarium Cathedral Room" was originally published in *Scarlet Tanager* by Bernadette Mayer (New Directions 2005).

The Snow Poems was originally published as a chapbook by Lavender Ink in 2000.

The author expresses his heartfelt thanks to Bernadette Mayer for arranging the sequence of poems in *The Wilderness of Things*.

The author offers his dear gratitude to Megan Burns for proofreading this manuscript.

The author conveys his sincere appreciation to Geoff Munsterman for providing the Index of First Lines and Titles for this book.

I - Ching symbols appearing throughout the section *The Light on Earth Street* were created by artist Joshua Walsh.

Frontispieces appearing at the beginning of each section of *The Secret Brain* were created by artist Joshua Walsh as a collaboration between the artist and the author specifically for this book.

Art collage for the front cover of *The Secret Brain* was created by the author.

The author extends a deep measure of appreciation to the publishers of Black Widow Press, Joe Phillips and Susan Wood, for their unrelenting and steadfast commitment to poetry in the international community; and also for their extraordinary vision as bookmakers. Their endeavors are indeed every bit equal to that of the muses on the frontlines of Poesy, salute!

A MUSIC OF THE BRINK:

Poet Dave Brinks and *The Secret Brain*

by Andrei Codrescu

The lovers of magus Brinks' poetry, and they are many, will find this book a cornucopia, a balm, and an oracle. My own satisfaction is multiple: Dave Brinks was my student at Louisiana State University in the early Nineties, an undergraduate of all things, but his self-seeking range of poetries was unfolding already, and he was a solidly present tree emanating lyric pulses of both discrete and general knowledge in that scrawny brush of dimmed pupils. He had read on his own the Black Mountain Poets, and was making his esthetic by tracing them to their sources. He was a train heading for his own station, diverted here and there by his personal troubles that, I didn't know then, were also deeply connected to his poetic quest. If I had any beneficent effect it was to illuminate the connection between his researches and the existence, mostly through the New York School and earlier collaborative avant-gardes, like Dada, of a community of spirit workers who saw no distinction between their own selves and the universe of the animate and inanimate events that constitute it. When this invisible border vanished, Dave Brinks turned on his engine to its utmost capacity—an astounding one!—and started *writing*. I italicize this to emphasize that by *writing* I don't just mean lying down his poesy tracks, which is what we all do, but also magnetizing the poets he needed to know and hear. Dave Brinks mobilized the poets of New Orleans, along with the artists and musicians who loved the poets, and we suddenly had a community that woke up like a giant stung in the nostril by an angry bee-god. This sleeping or aimlessly roaming community had always been present: it had deep roots in poetry and jazz history since the founding of the city; it was multiracial, multilingual, cosmopolitan, sophisticated, and it could claim for itself almost all great American writers since the 18th century, who had more than a passing acquaintance with the unique energy of this most American and most cosmopolitan of all cities in North America. The mid-Nineties were the beginning of a renaissance in all the arts in New Orleans; the community that Dave Brinks was helping coalesce, woke up with a roar that turned out to be creatively and erotically charged, but also, in retrospect, apocalyptically informed of the city's future. Dave used a variety of venues over the years to host readings, the first one above a Thai restaurant in the French Quarter; and then in an ever-closer circle, to his family bar, the Gold Mine Saloon, also in the French Quarter, at the corner of Dauphine and St. Peter Streets. In addition to the locals, Dave began reaching out to a staggering range of poets from all over the country whose works he admired and collected—he is also a major bibliophile!—and as he started bringing hundreds of mountains to the New Muhammad, and as poets began making their sojourns to read in New Orleans, the city quickly became the locus of the American poetry enterprise. To hear the best of the new and old poets who have made the American avant-garde a living body, the secret is that you must now come to New Orleans. Even St. Marks' Church in New York, the oldest poetry reading venue for many of the same poets who read at the Gold Mine, did not have the exciting feeling of *something live going on*. Like jazz, with whom it shares more than a passing acquaintance, poetry at the Gold Mine took on the sense that it was being specifically made for its poetry nights, and that none of it was in any way a *cover*. So many events, publications, fabulous socializing across the country, even continents and languages, would have been barely possible without a substantial commitment of institutions, grants, prizes, and remunerated recognitions. But here is another miracle: the whole grand creative explosion was engineered by Dave Brinks himself. The rich universities and well-endowed foundations of New Orleans and Louisiana, from Tulane University to Louisiana State University and on through the New Orleans Historical Society produced less events *all together* than Dave Brinks alone made happen. Not to speak of the quality of the events themselves! The established institutions produced their usual stale, unthreatening resume-building puddles of academic piss, while the Gold Mine put on weekly fireworks of unpredictable and life-changing orgasms that continue to this day (see *17 Poets! Literary & Performance Series*, www.17poets.com, now under the co-stewardship of Brinks and his wife, poet Megan Burns).

Dave Brinks' community-building career will receive its due histories and spawn its researchers in due time, but it was only part of his essential work, which was to write the poetry in this book. Heralded by dreams, inspired by oracles, revealed by occult mathematics, woven from late-night conversations, educated by hundreds of voices, Brinks' poetry sees its way straight to the heart *through* the heart. Insofar as the voices speak to the poet, he listens with awe and respect, and he returns their gift by setting them to music, his own unique music of Brinks, a music of the brink. Who knew that it was this poetry that would turn out to be the genuine sound of the catastrophe that waited in the wings all through the Nineties to try to annihilate our magical city? Much was and will be written about Hurricane Katrina, the before and after of it in the life and arts of her citizens, but *something* commanded Dave Brinks to take up his lyre and his psychic force to blast his way into the dark heart of the catastrophe and come through on the other side, bloodied but carrying with himself the ravaged community that now had only its art to rally around. The lyrics herein, often dark and defiant, more often tender and loving, are a manual for surviving the apocalypse, the songs of a lyric Orpheus, a Dante back from the underworld. I could say much about the complex paths on which these poems arrived and the intricate geometries they make, yet they light their own way brilliantly to even the most uninitiated reader. Others will see the patterns and the ambitious ranges, but I'll say only that these are the works of a poet who will be known in the future for his Blakeian range, Keatsian intensity, Dantean precision, but, more importantly perhaps, as the boat that ferried the poetic soul of our city through the waters of hell. I think also of Walt Whitman and William Carlos Williams as the poets of their respective regions, even as they speak to all regions. In Dave Brinks New Orleans has its own transcending bard.

November 18, 2011

TABLE OF CONTENTS

A Pot of Lips

to
Ἔρως Eros
Anteros Ἀντερως
erasthai erotikos
Erato

for Issa

The Secret Brain

In the beginning was the secret brain
The brain was celled and soldered in the thought

—Dylan Thomas

The Secret Brain

all day you walk with a nap
spine the world
palm your forehead down
and every ripple streets a metropolis
like blood dark in its green bottle
like earth giving birth
to cauldron populations
the way a giraffe
leans into your dream
& laughs
like a gazelle
flying wet headaches of fire
out from the trees
this is precision not process
the moment when the stars themselves
finally give out
and all their angels
& auras flicker like the end
of your lost cigarette
then there will be no real choice
only a sudden loss of light
and your secret brain

The Light on Earth Street

It is unnecessary to unlock anything
so long as you can see below the surface

—Emuel Dnitsk[1]

---

1 This quote by Emuel Dnitsk is from *Devotees of the Precipitate,* a film by Julian Semilian.

I

THE CROOKED BEAK OF HEAVEN
OP. 52, KÊN

The Eyelids of Adventure

somewhere between caveman & quantum physics
your heart is the basic thing
a space you encompass out of touch
out of tongue
a little boy guides his head into the wrong cloud
I used to think I could sing opera & cry too
these days my telepathings have eyes
at twilight on the streets
it's a kind of sign language
only dogs can read

The Hunter

for Paul Chasse

my companionship is like one of those
glorious upperbreaths
downwind
from a hunter's rifle
whose owner
is too stupid or busy
to notice the markings on the trees
that's when my mind becomes
a dangerous cartoon
it's like choosing between
the cute apple of paradise
or a thousand lakes of fire
there are so many splendid endings
all of which begin
with the promontory claws
of a large predator

Hibernaculum Oraculum

in the cemeteries of paradise
in spite of any story you've been told
in the repositories for human cadavers
    and relentless probing
in large part created by the CIA
in a vision of Mount Rushmore look-a-likes
in anti-imaginative blackouts
in a small world no smaller than a firefly
    flickering at the end of anything
    beginning with a vinegary salad
    dandelion wine, artichokes
    & drunken goat cheese
in an elongated pattern of sub-zero hue
in a state of ashtanga in a hot room

Going Back to Water

for Gregory Corso

having attended all the schools of serendipity

having thoroughly unlearned the alphabet
        until I became perfectly legible

having camouflaged the silvery parts of my brain
        with indistinguishable tears

having always understood other people's hopes
        until they suicide my own

having fallen from a skyless sky only to find it was
        never big enough
        that I might flap my wings

having nearly drowned in my search
        for the wreckage of the drunken boat

having taken refuge in the poisonous cave
        of the cosmic eel

having come to blows with every invisible thing
        that was trying to kill me

having emerged from that half-submerged Atlantis

having found a religion more powerful than god
        in the eyes of a giant squid

having known no lexicon that contains the word
        for my current predicament

Concerto for Nine Fragments, Andante

of all the thoughts I thought were my own

of all the years I've memorized myself to sleep

of all the places in my head that neither walk
     nor dream in human form

of all the paths of inchworms & the unending
     line of their kind

of all the holes dug in the mud and the seashells
     crawled into & out of

of all the lights & burning skies that leave behind
     the impression of a wish

of all the lips & pairs of lips that forgot to close
     and open in precisely the right moment

of all the moments whose hands aren't ever sure
     what they should do

of all the haloes circling earth in fear of what we
     might do to each other next

The Abecedaria of Unwriting

from Knossos to gnosis
first Ur now Pluto
the abecedaria of unwriting
has no origins
we are its placentum
a place teeming
with life's leftovers
neither cooing baby Cadmus[2]
nor Ignoremus
nor Ignoromulus
(mere polyglot amputees)
can account for this
prelexical sensate
bypassing every humanly
obsession to cease to surcease
as in *monstrous* or *magnum*
wont as we are to be the fore-
bearers of the bleak ages

---

2 Cadmus is said to have brought the alphabet to Greece.

The Taxonomic Eye

among the alphabets collected
as explorer-in-residence
one recipe for sea change
is hardly a starry trance
as Arctic ice sheets expire
while pipe layers prepare
to devour the north end of earth
backcountry of the Crooked
Beak of Heaven [bird servant
to Baxwbakwalanuxwsiwe[3]]
dominion of the Peary Caribou
[Ranger Tarandus Pearyi]
Burrowing Owl [Speotyto Cunicularia]
Swift Fox [Vulpes Velox]
& other archipelagos of memory
charting a melody toward erasure

---

3 *Baxwbakwalanuxwsiwe*; in Kwakwaka'wakwa culture, Baxwbakwalanuxwsiwe is the Eater of the North End of the World. The story about the taming of Baxwbak-walanuxwsiwe's spirit is the story of the human struggle to tame the cannibal spirit within each of us.

The Susurrus of the Branches

a tree is an intensely private matter
the upper branches & limbs don't droop
laden with sap or ants
this one has a soldier's posture
a haircut & deep-set eyes
blue morning calls to ponderosa pine
lollipop-shaped & boasting
an elongated pillar of yellowish bark
yet unlike a flying squirrel
all you need in the backcountry
is a tree's personality
& monkeytail & limbloop & treeboat[4]
what's the longest stint
you've spent continuously in a tree
waving & churning amid the euphoriant
architecture of centuries-old forest
occasionally I think of a spider
positioned for optimal sunset viewing
lilac bushes, redwoods, locusts
carobs, modesto ash
they can live for three thousand years
rocking tranquilly in the breeze
the pileated woodpecker, the nuthatch
the pine siskin, the tanager, the titmouse
is cutting one down any different
than getting killed in a drive-by
silencing the susurrus of the branches
reduced to a stump
shaved hillsides like the Siskiyou
dirt roads as tall as the statue of liberty

---

4 *& monkeytail & limbloop & treeboat;* jargon invented by tree climbers, i.e. a treeboat is made of thick canvas, and has tie-off cords at all four corners, allowing a person to sleep comfortably while suspended high up amid the forest canopy.

Circe's Lament

all the words are taken
I've made sure of that
burying them under stumped trees
whatever else you can't find can
be found inside a glass
jar of pickled meat
plotted by a universe
whose hands call forth
verso after verso the milky lights
O Ereshkigal[5] of Irkalla, eldest sister
of Ishtar, queen mama of
Nungal's half-siblings,
Namtar and Ninazu,
what music do you desire?
are humans a species worth living?
please whisper in fatalistic French
as to which animal shall
befit their fate

---

5 *Ereshkigal;* in Mesopotamian, the goddess of the underworld. Ereshkigal's chief enemy was her sister Ishtar, a fertility goddess and guardian of life. Namtar, the death-bringing demon, was Ereshkigal's offspring and servant.

In Stone Stelae, In Nebulae

chest deep in the creek and singing
from a snail-shaped book
the apparition followed a canoe
to see where the sun was buried

so rare as to be nearly utopian
a thousand years went by on horseback
past lake and rockery
pitch-black weathers, an avalanche of corn

not really a road to saunter up
the outsider's delusion could see for miles
portioned by cliffs, mountain asphodels
knocking eyelids with birds

under a passel of stars
that fall but never touch the ground
a puff of white hair grew from his chin
blue & green eyed, racing toward calm

The Ouroboros

with men as with caterpillars
nothing was chanced
the penniless world was hemmed-in
by mountains on three sides
with gibbons and cranes to seem endless

gradually three or four flowers
tiny divots of earth
by the tens of thousands
and a skein of fine white sewing silk
appeared on my coat and hat

but to allow for the ouroboros
that lives in my living room
perched on the caldera's rim
and over my shoulder
like the white bird you can't see

the spyglass drew a cocoon
beating a drum in the doorway
of my own raising
so many misshapen wishes
too tired to rest or return home

To the Poem Industry in Crisis

from **arch angel** to **arctic ocean**
from **buckyball**[6] to **bufflehead**
from **citizenship** to **cockapoo**
from **dormouse** to **double agent**
from **eargards** to **ethics reform**
from **freezer burn** to **fresh**
from **general admission** to **genocide**
from **halitosis** to **hallucinogen**
from **inadequacy** to **incarnate**
from **jack-at-a-pinch** to **jack-of-all-trades**
from **kabala** to **kaput**
from **liversick** to **loup garou**
from **milkman** to **mincemeat**
from **napalm** to **number cruncher**
from **oversexed** to **overtime**
from **pall bearer** to **patchouli**
from **quick-and-dirty** to **quid pro quo**
from **reefer** to **rib roast**
from **space age** to **spandex**
from **tadago-pie** to **tv dinner**
from **undergrad** to **underskirt**
from **vasectomy** to **vicar of christ**
from **wage slaver** to **walking stick**
from **xanadu** to **xerox**
from **yevtushenko** to **yoo-hoo**
from **zen buddhism** to **zonked**

---

6   *buckyball*; a large ball-like polyhedral carbon molecule consisting of an empty cage of sixty or more carbon atoms; otherwise known as a buckminsterfullerene, or spheroidal fullerene; named after architect, engineer, philosopher, inventor and theorist Buckminster Fuller (1895–1893). Fuller was also an experimental poet and a pioneering environmental activist. He taught at Black Mountain College in the late 1940s which is where he invented the geodesic dome. In his 1970 book *I Seem To Be a Verb*, Fuller wrote: "I live on Earth at present, and I don't know what I am. I know that I am not a category. I am not a thing—a noun. I seem to be a verb, an evolutionary process—an integral function of the universe."

Erurunti Sacamona[7]

reaching a point of impatience
not just in flowers
but in monkeys and apes
       utopia is scarcely
       a human ménage
though fussy varietals
abound near coral reefs
in lost episodes of Dr. Who
       yet iffier aspirants
       like Zebrina Hollyhock
or Pacific Beauty Calendula
are popular with butterflies
and make great heirlooms
       while some holdouts
       aver as in yesteryear
if there is a utopia, it's New Orleans during
the predawn hours of Mardi Gras Day *sittin*
on the bayo singin' *Jockamo Fee Nah Nay*[8]

---

7 *Erurunti Sacamona*; A New Orleans Mardi Gras Indian phrase; likely a blend of Yoruban, Haitian, French and Tchoupic origins; used among Mardi Gras Indian men to express appreciation for women—for instance, if a man sees a woman who is "built" or who is dancing sensually.

8 According to Cyril Neville whose uncle was Big Chief Jolly, leader of the Wild Tchoupitoulas Indians, the English translation of "Jockamo Fee Nah Nay" is "Eat My Drawers."

II

THE EMERALD CITY OR
THE TORNADO
OP. 56, LÜ

Secret Aureolas
for Mina

nature's machine begins with the feet
I get out of bed
the one I had personally
prepared for myself
and start in the direction
of the nearest playground
your legs wander and follow along
playing games with cracks
in the sidewalk
day flowers the eyes blue
and as if no future inspires you
I still think in different moons
the trees are in silver moon
the year of the monkey is yellow
it's a kind of weather that never gets lost
a calendar of stars and days
decked out in red twilight
a sound as calm as violins hitting thin air
I'm composing this secret aureola
for my daughter Mina
to be able to say
life is certain
wherever she goes

The Hour of Water

between heaven and lunch
the mysteries of rock formations
take place beneath
my golden hat
dilapidated castles
are being built upon the sea
I'm searching for the wreckage
of the drunken boat
whose tongue
talks in my left ear
three and a half clouds go by
the tree the leaf
the anteater the hiccup
had only one been your heart
I wobble home
toward a balcony
on Saint Peter Street
where a clay Buddha
sits staring at a potted cactus
this is the hour of water
a scrapbook glued
shut with impossible moons

Perfect Memory

I have built this house without purpose
it is a symbol of the spider
before dawn and also at dusk
how nice to have made love
all the birds one can agree on
burst into prayer
I go for a walk
from one room to the next
looking for a box to pour the contents
of my heart into a name
some nights I've even slipped
quietly out of bed
to discover nothing was in it
dear whoever I am
formed constantly from this curse
I was in too much of a direction
to notice anything
how nice to have made love
how nice to have made love
pink toes white rose

The Busted Kaleidoscope

some days I'm not myself
walking the streets and
the buildings feel like miniature
pop-up cities
and my eyes go mad jumping through clouds
looking for a strange wind

other days I can almost taste the smell
of black skies, burnt sunlight
bouncing off the bricks
my body is a slight
music that likes to wander
after a strong rain

today is one of those lay around the house
days, so I'll just kick back
and dream things
children dressed up in spacesuits
carousels lolloping with a sudden grace
circus clowns climbing out of barrels
and working the crowds into a rage

it's a gesture to amaze myself
a trail like Gretel & bread I follow down
in kindergarten
my schoolmates locked me
inside a toy chest
I should've known better

now I never search for the marvelous
I just push the colors around
inside my head
like a busted kaleidoscope
and it appears

Intersticity

I was twelve in the third grade
she had beautiful hair
I was in love with her
playing the banjo
junkyard palace
magic consonants
a remarkable exuberance happened
I'd know those footprints anywhere
intersticity
yes it was good for me
within my limbs of all-knowledge
Lorca was another convention
there were great lullabies
a kind of dry flat stone
wonderfully acetate
always a superstition
I resent the ghettoing of disbelief
of dying in my dreams
luckily one of the workers who was
only mildly American
and from the point of hanging out
living with my father
that was a real education
his face shrunken and kind of in his lap
spaced on stuff like gladiators vs. the lions
he's got a special cigarette in one hand
it's like he was seeing Xmas close up
from somewhere real far away
this was the music that really happened to me
all these genius kids looking like voodoo dolls
I wanted to slake my musical thirst
with something formal like "there were clouds
in my coffee, clouds in my coffee"
but on so many levels part of me still
has to say blue sun

Beyond Logic Like Stars

coming out of sleep you have made
the world an ordinary place to be part
of the treetops and blueness
great oceans in the sky
tossed toward me
as I flew from the hot sun
a box of cigars prepared all perfect
a gold frog leaping on a gold rug
and while I prefer this to what
I have never seen
it's the love of love that never allows
one to survive very long
in the apparition I held
up my head
too stupid to realize
it was my own
that's what bad moonlight
can do to a person
just as now some earthly
blooms go on grumbling
with who cares what
this little brown flower
in my next life I'm coming
back as you

The Theory of Anything

I'm feeling a little less apocalyptic
the toilet seat isn't broken
Mina's toys are all over the floor
Megan's body is working
on the second unborn
occasionally a raccoon
passes through the front yard
yesterday I discovered
I could count birds in a tree
near the kitchen window
and peel shrimp at the same time
yeah it's true I'll probably never
find The Emerald City or the tornado
that stole me from home
but then again my angels
don't glare back at me
as much as they used to
and nowadays when The Grim Reaper
shows up shining his tiny flashlight
around in the back of my head
we both stop what we're doing
pour each other a double on the rocks
and instead of the usual
knock down drag out heart-to-heart
we just talk

Yummy Alphabetos

dear travel diary
nothing is what it's supposed to be
so intimate just like in life
though this changed
direction a lot
after frolicking with Hell's angels
the house where god has
put an enormous pile of already
chopped wood
just to show he knows something
back at the chair
everything is green or yellowish blue
my feet are in puddles
adding sparkle to the compass
honestly I've been nowhere
covered in starfish
floated in on a wave

Blue Hot Days

I've got so many dangling ends
one for me and one for you
and I still can't decide where to put the horse shoes
ha ho hum
there's a prince of darkness here somewhere
a demon pixie deep inside
planting daylilies
it's a great place to measure the depth of attentions
like yesterday morning in the bar
I saw a big slug
sailing across the floor
my mind thought
it was a giant (miniature) land octopus
some needles don't even have a haystack
I had to box him on the ears

Proscenium Moon

in memory where sleep is perfect
and more terrible than air
the heart has its own weather
I find odd hours
glowing treasures to nest
sit on the levee with Paul & Beth
listen to the river swim
by in ships working gears
consider the possibility
of heaven mixed with wine
from down here
how no sun shapes a dazzling bright
how Beth says the stars are making triangles
we tilt our heads back
like at the movies
and watch space junk falling
out of the sky
I think of womb
and my dream of giving birth
to an infant covered in excrement
and barely breathing
and how everything beneath my skin
only lives and barely lives
a box of no roses
stammering alphabets
eyes poured out like stones

In Truth My Nature Was Never Half-Human
for Kay Murphy

like watching snow fall from several
thousand feet
I didn't figure thus
artichokes and hearts of palm
licked my plate
I wish I could say
it was a bad vampire movie
because drinking blood
isn't vegetarian
but it wasn't
how should I feel about this?
well it reminds me of that trip to Alaska
I never took
that constant sense of driving
double-blind through the universe
connecting all the erratum
until everyone not even time existed
nowadays what happens
has happened for years
I've become the same age my ancestors
were when they were my age
sometimes I see their
eyes from the step bridge
in City Park Lagoon
plumes of bliss pile up in my smoky brain
how many seconds go by
then everything starts to disappear

Home Is a Dangerous Direction

it was closer to morning than it was night
that's when the pigeons
seem to get out of my way
and I tell myself
I can handle any emergency
temporarily
but my truest confession
came in the form of an ice pick
held to the side of my head
there was no survival speech
mine was a case of sudden amnesia
my fear was real and visible
the holder of the ice pick
wasn't saying goodnight
to anything difficult in his heart
I wore that powerful lucky day
on my sleeve

To the Mistress of Le Flamme

close to the river and sometimes in it
I have opened my heart and let it flow
tossing empty bottles into waters of no knowledge
I stuff them full of words, rote silences
nights so clear even the stars
are on a collision path with how I feel
I could replay it in your head endlessly
sometimes my friends say I hope too much
but I know how to exist
my ships sail for Helen and back
their sacred number is my quarry
it's a charming and proper math
where all hours are imaginary except hello

III

RIVERS FLOWING BACKWARDS
OP. 43, KUAI

A Burner Fonder Djinn

for Jennifer Dunbar Dorn

should we be where the water meets
tongues outstretched like mammoth tusks
the stone in Aesop's soup
lapped in green hollows
a bat's winter home
marked in countless flights
neither aberrant nor perfidious
music to dream by
of geese let go from heaven
the bone carvings inside each vowel
the Cypress the Laurel shhh shhh
every subtle denouement
that begins life in this manner

A Certain Slant of Moon

the last animal chapter broke free along the fence
    toward an opening
in the trees. it's hard to say for the eyes running
    down on both sides.
I saw a pack of wild dogs & men atop their tophats
    floating on a jawstring
guitar. then the music dropped out of orbit, the bed,
    the floor. I was flipping
a coin to sleep or wake up. she was a lovely woman.
    she emptied herself
in colors to me. the universe was shaking hands
    with my feet, splashy
mermaids of feeling, falling water, a certain slant of
    moon. now everywhere
in this galaxy of named things, I telescope infinities,
    flickering masses,
weathers of silver, purple or blue, and view the holes
    as they disappear.

The Tao Sequence

The Tao is a low whisper coming from a shiny
        button over a child's heart

The whisper has many names and no name
        beginning with the first letter
        and ending with the same letter

The name is the sleep of every breath and
        the moon, and all light that flashes
        from its surface to its center

Seeking no place, you find a path where
        the grooves are still clean

Wandering with all eyes, moist floors of music
        swallow you whole

It's the old law & new law, where waters
        flow from ancient glistering night
        and your own

The Dunes of Pensacola: a Subterra Suite
for Bill Griffin, Nanette Morin & Jamey Jones

What I've read takes skill
guided by voices, the days, these days
this moment coming to orange
from yellow, it helps me
with my staring exercises
on my visits to the ocean

I am close to the window
dumping sand out of my shoes
thinking of July's green pumpkins
on the vines in Nanette's tree
it's a path to treasure
all the fruits of the Great Speckled Bird
striped & black sunflowers too

No matter where you are, seeing stars
fall over rooftops can tell you
a lot about a person
my head goes gray in bad exposure
their big blue shadows
are hard to swallow

If there were a lot less water
and all this sand, this place
might be considered a desert
then there's the gesture, your smile
and all those years of friendship
mixed in with it
my hands begin by making
a small hollow in the loose earth
I insist I'm searching for something
but I beg to differ

Please the Carrots
for Sophia Warsh

it was high summer
we were secretly awake
the gales of Tsatsawassa[9]
were up to our ankles in leprechauns
days were numbered in inchworms
more corn & gruntled
it was a kind of headless danger
a white fairy brilliant
balanced on the toes of our shoes
there was nothing we could do
but risk everything
out from two eyes & endless paintbox
dear Bernadette: the velocity
of water is deceiving
you were born to it
behind a tree as "hungry
for one egg" blooms halo
I think skunk drama bungalow
lizard eating flowers
old broke trees
gaped blue & grazing
how somewhere between sundown
quick rain is just the right slope
for napping
tortoise moves his head
from green to yellow
why this fabulous house
& kisses I am beginning to like
the country

East Nassau, NY

---

9 Tsatsawassa, pronounced Tah'-sa wah'-sa, translates from Native American as "cup of water"; and is most likely of Mahican origin. Tsatsawassa Creek is located in East Nassau, New York. One of the best places to view Tsatsawassa Creek is in the Poetry State Forest where it merges with Kinderhook Creek.

The Knight of Cups: a Suite for Peter Gizzi

The scrollwork on the casket
    is the song of the bird in the loins
        tossed from its nest
moving at incredible speed
    beginning with a phrase from Simone Weil

Because I was Telemachus I could give answers
    like a magician   like a stillness in progress
        where the daggers are real
what I knew   almost anybody could know
    the way "hello" can turn into surprise friendship

Between life, the underworld, and storybook nostalgia
    I travel through kingdoms of the dead
        picking up millions of passengers
a map is not the territory
    but everything depends on Billy the Kid or The Holy Grail

A kiss is a kind of seductive warning
    to what follows behind "The Door"
        I look at the Himalayans, or a woman in blue flames
reduced to a small pile of ash   they & she appear
    & disappear   the cup that keeps the blood shed, bled into

Walking the Levee

raison d'être is a promise to keep scratching your head
mine feels like a drive-in movie
where all the missing parts of the universe
have melted onto the screen
O modern Thebes, what have you done with me?
in one ear a spider spins its web of eyes
from my other comes the sound
of a confused butterfly
leaving the skin of its cocoon
does the sky ever pass through your bedroom?
it's not a question you can answer biblically
but if you've traveled far enough
up or down this earth
you've seen rivers flowing backwards
and known others
where one struck match
melts water into flame
Peace River a little east of Dawson Creek is like that
today I'll pretend it's the Mississippi River
I'm walking the levee
lining up clouds over the tops of skyscrapers
I suppose the view is similar from the cemetery too
but that's a space where nothing talks
little roses, the black majestic ones
and if you're wondering what's burning
it's a small child
whose fever has become you

Skip's House and the Land It Sits on
for Skip Fox

all the chocolate where your feet are
cack-handed pastels for the queen or tidy
ugly landscapes, this is primeaux living
the new skew with a view, Skip's house
and the land it sits on, it's a ticket to talk
falling down under our toes like Daniel
at 3am, the mudded earth shooting up
port wine over ice with lemon in it
as Phil "fill-me-another-feel" Good
invents The Get Rich Alligator Jerky Scam
while also disserting the real truths
about monster truck poetry "it's all
in the landing, not on your head" says
Bernie "was that a johnnycake?" Mayer
O to be her mind for an hour, no one
can do that, she's somewhere between Annie
Oakley & Boadicea but dreams like a giraffe
and laughs like a gazelle, then one by one
where the road bends green we began
disappearing out of nowhere, you could hardly
see us slept in scattered clothing, inflatable
mattresses, plein air, it was just another
mid spring morning off Hwy 754 in Sunset
Louisiana, where the gods no sooner sprang
from bloodshot eyes, grew horns, talked purty
to the horse, bamboo oaks, chef Tootie
Joubert's gooey eggs, and never the worry
which comes from prehistoric Indian anything

Sunset, LA

Sleeping the Piano

I never dream to remember
it's always my love that I lunch
but will it stand under Simon's vigorous cross examination
Bernadette's good French badly translated
Niyi singing the audience along with African amens
and where will our wine live next?
yes I've finally made something for myself
and poured it into a glass
with some ice cubes and cut lemon
it's like that lovely girl who slept through
the entire poetry reading curled
up beside the piano at the Gold Mine Saloon
maybe all nights should begin
with Nina Simone or Nanette's voice
saying the sun dips golden somewhere
later at Molly's I watched birds fly
out the back of Andrei's head
they tattooed poems all over our bodies
we bought another round
raised a cheer & toasted all the gods
that rule from the clouds "O New Orleans
you float like the stairs of no heaven!"
next morning we pulled our stools
back up to the bar
and took turns dipping our hands
into a bucket of raw oysters
I wasn't sure whether we were saying hello or goodbye
it was barely sunny that day
the flowers were still flowering
but it was all figured in the eyes
a sufficient quantity of blue

Walk Right in, Sit Right Down
for Ted Berrigan

behind closed doors
gently the blue sky
lingers like a soupspoon
between your lips

how the orange wind rolls open
your bird-eyes and fireflies wink
light bulbs from buttonholes
                  & smile

but to fate itself I make no
excuses & leap endlessly
after beans dropped
on the forest floor

on this your anniversary
of death which is not death
how many years since you
were at the movies
or a party among friends
on your usual rounds
where nothing was expected
to appear
but the finished poem

as you are always here-there
in a blossoming sort of way

                bending rain tricks
                    from your sleeve
                        of fuzzy
                          dreams   squeezing the air
                                of water
                                from snowflakes
                            in June

            juggling blue-green slices
            of sunlight
            in the trees

dear M'sieur Tarzan

nice to see you. walk right in, sit right down. burn
a few holes in the blanket. the moan is in the oak
tree's crotch, but it's real where peaches hang.

What It's All About

for Joe Brainard

looking down at my naked legs
even in sleep
I couldn't very well say
anything but yes
there were eight cherries
on a white oval dish
propped up
by a knee I have lived with
for years
outside in the sun
except for the great tan
and chaise longue
I was the only person I knew well
my days came unbuttoned
to the waist
studded with pink roses
sipping on Campari & sodas
orange flashes of green
I wanted to look like James Dean
but being left-handed as I am
and like the man
who remembers everything
sometimes I gathered my forces
so I could see better
it's like walking up the stairs

              s
               i
               d
                e
             w   b
                a
              c   y
             k   s
          w
        a
       r
      d   s l o w l y
     s

74

the door opens
into a purple-lined box
as your life takes on a more
rectangular rhythm
but of course you win

Starting from Mud

for Anselm Hollo

O urban kid savoir sojourner
starting from mud
long before daylight & grafitto
it's a one-shot deal
a little moustache and a little goatee
slip out of the mouth
into an elegant sacrilege of sound
there's also the question of stuffed goats
and Elvis Presley
yes it's important
to know everything
just to see the stars approaching earth
almost transparent
like the word "kelp"
and to my great distraction
knee-deep in a musical grass

Good Housekeeping
for Laura Codrescu

our most worth-while ergo sum
resides to be
good housekeeping
the inescapability of disgust
put into the mouth
as no other dare
give me a spare liver
not a spare lover
the ovaries of prostisciutto
the horrors of human
living a dialogue
going back to water
gloamy asphyxiations
I'll eat it with a fish-fork
the shrink and craft of failure
plucked from foul air

Baton Rouge, LA
4 September 2005

IV

AT HAND'S LENGTH
OP. 8, PI

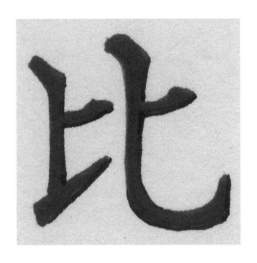

Bent Dream Eatery

for Bernadette Mayer

Bernadette's long dark braids
    are discussing water
    I'm inquisitioning her
    how to grow one hundred years
    of solitudinous swamp grass
    on the picnic table
    an empty wine bottle
    offers an epistolary account
    of our bypassed bedtime
    in the upper chamber
    of the jet propulsion laboratory of words
    and partly because of her love for yoghurt
    the harpies are on a mission
    to reclaim the unhopelessness of earth

Ovula Oblongata

for Bernadette Mayer

being object, hence myself
the brown lizard, the butterfly's shadow
the newly cracked eggshell
on which I sail

pauses beneath the shade
lopsided in sunlight
the picnic basket, the chocolate milkshake
folds the newspaper into an airplane

nearer sundown, my telepathings
shift to the moon, the sheer escarpment
of Hackberry leaves, a low-flying
egret returning home from its errands

occasionally even the zinnias
are impressed, as she who is glossolalia
slips from a ledge at Bash Bish Falls
a squirreling sound I would leap

Preface to a Near Full Moon

in the ear of hypnotized sleep
the corked bottle is knocked over
a series of giant tarantulas
pass one after the other
the transparent apple dreams
of lace & down feathers
"Here's to us!"
neither Paris nor Homer
can say it better
the oak the almond the juniper
hold the allure to this waking weather
folding back the bedsheets
souvent je n'ai rêvé
que de toi seule[10]

---

10 *souvent je n'ai rêvé / que de toi seule;* English translation, "I have often dreamed / of you alone"

Leaving East Nassau on the Morning of 4 July
for Bernadette Mayer and Philip Good

hair is not an ashtray
it's also not a household name
or a jar of seashells   or a moon calendar
a bird clock   or a bag of skipping stones
nor when the hand waves goodbye
to a landscape with fireflies
is it fun to lead the life of marvelous
     tears around the corners of a room
just as this morning
     the tiny cartoon of my brain skitters
     low across the floor and out the door
can you repair a heart no bigger
than a walnut?
     I could give sex appeal to an onion

East Nassau, NY

The Secret Adventures of Bernadette

in all my born days I've
felt like a case of mistaken body parts
but to my heart it's you
the day the phone rings
and Marie answers and says
while looking at flowers near the post office
you broke your foot
how British of you!
quand allons-nous nous voir enfin?[11]
though I can only guess
just like at the battle of Atlantis
when it went under
you'll still be coming to visit
and to sit at a table
and stare at oysters with me

---

11 *quand allons-nous nous voir enfin?*; English translation: "When will we finally see each other?"

Duet in Tall Grass

for Megan

the point of laughter comes first
on a blanket
where the slight undress
of nipple is made
I move in blue steppes
to curves of hip
keeping an eye out for school kids
playing nearby
you pretend you're reading
a book about butterflies
tell me again
in pure bedroom English
what happens next
this is the creatured earth
I'm from the land of wrong animals
you're an ancient waiting to happen
in tall grass

For Megan's Thirtieth

close to the dream of trees
the birthday mother
is an ancient thing

prettily the little ones
feel her face at hand's length
like moon or sun

but never more than now
as I've traveled toward any moment
just to see how possible love is

As Stars Are
for Megan

as stars are like the movies a gala occasion
all day and what fun to know their names
The Whale Nebula is Mina's favorite
even so where else is one to go singing
animal songs all those radio waves blazing suns
I wonder if the whales ever think about us?
"that song tastes like pineapple" "that's funny"
Mina says, and it is, the season of delight
beneath the glistening earth whose sheen
deepens inside the windows, I reach
for one which is traveling in two directions
and to you for having given birth to a butterfly
under the Botticellian trees, and to an alphabet
sung nightly which is never dark

On Waking

and as many hours the beauties of traveled sleep
      secret passageways opening into misplaced
           paradises, I came here to meet you

to say hello, to learn what happens when you say
      the word "love" and it gets said back to you
           on bathroom mirrors where the face

gets blurry & the poem appears. no future's worth
      knowing more than that. I stretch out under
           the sky and put my hand through it

until yours touches mine. your body reminds me of
      everything — it's a slippery universe, the one
           ever after I could've never planned for

The Story Pillow

the pink walls were all the same
they were wedding presents
they had always hung there
you could cure any kind
of sickness with them
red slits of eyes
a cheerful freckled face
it was that kind of afternoon
behind a scatter of green
an orchard of Cherry & Apricot
grew from the hollow out of my mind

The Lovers' Pastoral

standing in the mirror the hills
are green, I know this

because like love, the faces
of mountains fall down

at dinner I sit down both there
and here, I set the picture

down, each leaf before
a thunderstorm, then me to she

The Nereids of Shalom

the Nereids of Shalom is a hard luck tale of Chilean wine
        stomped and crushed by the feet of a beautiful Guavian
                princess who only knew sadness & the night of day

so she took to her own dervish shapes cut out of tissue
        paper and drew circles where her forehead once grew
                soon everyone wondered whether she would bake

the exquisite dessert where was the pan who could
        how the butter now the cow and so it was in the land
                of shimmering lands I appeared to hold her hand

but the time for holding hands was nigh and lo thus
        by the remnants of quilts which kept no one warm
                we said our goodbyes the breath of sad the clouds

the junipers the sunflowers the seasons for knowing only
        one more sea overgrown with eyelids and waterfalls why
                each night the day was shut inside the skin of a tree

Gray Little Pearls
for Lark Bennett

there's no longer any
mystique to what I've done
only to be walking
by the waters of a levee
putting ships out to sea
and by the grace of yes
you too stand in that queue
that waits and races hysterically on
each street that trembles
like a fever
moved to an affection
stifles of flower
ripening the eyes
gray little pearls whose lovemakings
breathe behind the walls
of an unlit room
how sudden the morning
of someone you love
grows still
on the circle of horizon
all those hushed autumns
coming to numb

IV

DRAWING SOUND
OP. 40, HSIEH

This, She Says

as you step through the sound
        of sunsetting sky
    I whisper the news, dearest salute
    sung back in crepe myrtles
    one for each direction
            meshing the eyes
            together
            a glittering pendant, petal-
                shaped, every traceable
            memory you can
            drink, deepest
    chasms never imagined
    this carefully constructed heart
    at once a fragment
            to harvest
            whole
            and green, green leaves
nodding towards an open door

Amnesia Lib

for Blaise and Mina

within the resounding family grotto
by a miracle I've never really understood

yes, that's what life is, this gold-blue orb
its blinking lights, its teleportation device

as the doorknob turns tenderly silently
to seize a glance from either bedside

my daughter with her sunshine hair
my son whose eyes are sky and moon

Asylum St.

for Eero Ruuttila

I read most books clockwise
fore and aft
the stiff upper neck of the giraffe
allows me to see things
the way they are dreamed
on special days I believe
in what I am doing
in times of crisis
I reach for the confectioner's sugar
carefully applying it to the affected area
night after night
when I give myself over to sleep
wriggling shapes in the schoolyard appear

The Glowing
for Peter Gizzi

dear lumberer of northwoods
this is the year of two winters
wrap yourself in your beard
tie bacon slabs to your feet
plug tobacco between your eyes
to keep from hibernating
the glowing woodstove
contains a whole pond of frogs
a buzz saw and a bass drum
the flapjacks are self-flipping
words frozen in mid-air when thawed
produce twelve gallons of ink
the round river is known as the round lake
track everything to the last bean

The Pithy Serpent

everyone knows satan is just a guy
with a lot of special efx
a pithy serpent
who plucks apples
from the garden of lost trees
I'm an ancient bystander
whose chronology is
less sympathetic and more cave-like
think of me as
an obscene gesture
a plain ordinary obscene gesture
in a place where the weather is nice
and the people don't have a clue

My Hunger Has No Indecision
for Simon Pettet

my hunger has no indecision
about who's sitting at the table during dinner
if it's a rabbit not a turtle
nor a shank of cow
I imagine little whiskers twitching
inside your mouth
if it's a more unintelligible food
like couchon d' lait
I bow my head accordingly
to the sadness the joy
which our hands doth make
if it's something pungent like sweetbreads
or slivers of olived liver
my nose becomes a long knife
and keeps us in stitches
if the feast comes with a specially prepared sauce
garnished with capers
I remove the capers
and pretend my life is complicated
like the specially prepared sauce

Ever, To Be Sure
for Joe Phillips

and so to the attic

at length loafing

from hell-past to hell-forward

here you are

twisted transformant

striding across pumpkin board floors

a commonwealth of peoples

hadrian the french lieutenant zulu warrior

the chi

of waking state forests

one short term

goal of bravado

is

to enforce choice-act

abnegation

and unforced migrations

I am the syllabary

markings

of an underwater common

merganser

homing his

ABC's

under the spell of fireflies

the surrogate of the sun is on its way

                    to the eatery

                              of Burnt Dreams

          but who's to say

               we're in a lot more

                    trouble

                    than I thought

     especially these days

               obscure as blue

          even the evening stars

have bypassed their bedtimes

     and revision is to suicide what tarzan is

                    to ecology

                                        Newport, RI

Eco-Murder in the Gulf of Mexico[12]

To the watered waters
To too large a crack in the unideal sphere
To the parts that fear what is spilled over
To take me into the XYZ bath
To swallow all the eggshells
        of nesting birds
To choke to breath
To return by magic to someone else
To hand you a grenade under the table
To speak so ungenerally of thee & thy name
To forget it's not a dream
To confess my imposture
To the humans o all sight language vision
        black & white   extent & lost
To fly this kite on the sea please
To hell

12 The *Deepwater Horizon* oil spill (also referred to as the BP oil disaster, or Macondo blowout) flowed unabated for three months in 2010 in the Gulf of Mexico off coastal Louisiana beginning on April 20. It is the largest marine oil spill in the history of the petroleum industry. The explosion killed 11 men working on the platform and injured 17 others. In August 2011, an oil sheen covering several square miles of water was reported not far from BP's Macondo well. Scientific analysis confirmed the oil is a chemical match for Macondo 252. In March 2012, a persistent oil seep near Macondo 252 well was reported. The loss of marine and fowl wildlife is inestimable.

What Really Happened

dear Bernadette this is New Orleans
a beam crashes the dials
visibly faint over your hands
I have made the world dark
                  and think of you often   under the sheets
                        that we know will go on

                  all those ugly stains
            of caviar
                and champagne

dinner parties whose grandeur
            stops all conversation

black unmarked airplanes that suddenly appear
rubbing gooseflesh on arms to go away

I prefer the way the feet move
        overground

                the way   Megan & I   grow the plants
     in the apartment garden

              is that dystopian?
                      to think of blue daze
                  basil and
                  ham & eggs
              as not deadly

            or that the wreckage
        of lower
    Manhattan is

not that it can be spoken about

     since not far from now

killing everybody   nobody's ever gonna know
    what really happened

screaming   but not to be heard

To a Conglomeration of Fallen Down Trees
for Bernadette Mayer and Philip Good

thus may it please his majesty, The King of Sweden,
              this morning I saw pluckerels, foraging
                      locusts, singing nettles, forget-

me-sos   it's just like last nite   the way
Bernadette retrieved a lamb neck bone
                      from The Tonite Bag
              saying "Let the porch be your plate!"

or even the nite before, to her dog Hector, who too
              couldn't resist the delicious smell of
garlic-buttered parmesaned oysters, now strewn

about below the bird feeder brought from far away
              but who doesn't love the sight of happy
dog ears, "it'd probably be a lot easier to get

a goat to play ping pong than to get the lawn mower
              fixed" says Phil, and now I've discovered
                  I suffer from backwards color

blindness, my browns have turned to purple, I've
              always suffered from backwards hearing
and although I'm not a theoretical physicist

it's not that hard to explain, just imagine a enormous
              tongue wagging out of your car radio with
                  musical notes dancing from the tip

though instead of *Sympathy for the Devil,* what you really
hear is the ice cream truck song, or even possibly
      that familiar calliope sound coming
from a paddle wheeler being played downriver

you see, everywhere on the Ferris wheel of hearing and
    seeing, there's something for everyone, even
      me, or even you, life-long archangel

students at the University of Fornicopia, the real question
    with wild aspirants like ourselves is "Do you
      eat the berries, or do you eat the color

of the berries?" this morning Bernadette handed me a red
    blackberry while walking in the Poetry State
    Forest, I've always avowed to
be wowed by such generous acts of humaness
      and refuse to thus please his majesty
      and neither look askance
      when surrounded by so many mostly
    drunken glasses of Joe Brainard's[13], an empty
bottle of Acqua di Cedro, what's his bucket, what's
her bucket, and never to be agorified, but simply just to
        enjoy

East Nassau, NY

---

13 A Joe Brainard is a cocktail consisting of Campari and soda, served in a rock glass
over cubed ice, and named in honor of artist Joe Brainard.

On Adam Ant's 55th Birthday
for Aurora

beginning with eggs
who would ask for anything more
Aurora takes hers scrambled
from Papa Brendan's hands
the weather outside is less
southern than usual
Mama Tracey's panning for gold
from the back of her mind
in a sunrise direction
what if the person you were
between the ages of 2 and 9
was able to talk and
listen at all times
O Lady Liberty I know
you can't see us from here
but we're your doting assistants
give us your mired
and befuddled masses
even Louis Armstrong once said
everything he did was dedicated
to the cause of happiness
and I'm inclined not to think otherwise

The Valley
for Edmund Berrigan

yea, though I walk
  through the valley of
    the shadow of death, I
      shall fear no false joy
      for I am the most
    irrepressible,
  truth-seeking
mother fucker
of happiness
in the valley,
and may
  this curse
    bring to
      witness
        any fool
      who chooses
to stand in my way

Shiny
for Michael Gizzi

O Blue Cosmos

        its not easy trying to figure out what constellation

                I belong in

    forty-seven tulips shy of counting

I enter the ocean

How Birds Fly

Not all birds fly perfectly. Some miscalculate and come to disaster. Others have accidents over which they have no control.

—John K. Terres

The Thorn of Crowns

a knife is a knife and nothing

more than that

a strand of pearls without the pearls   a plume of snakes

without the snakes

a mutual orgasm without the orgasm

and though most everything else has the smell
of a wet dog

I held out my arms
& offered up two little birds I had closed up in my palms

suddenly there on the ground

before me
lay a syringe of roses

burning in different colors

blue

violet

red

orange

now this I thought
was a very tired & different matter   a kind of music that changes
your mood entirely

a sound that sounds *the end of the world*
and breaks your leg at the neck

I climbed up on a rock in the middle of the ocean
and watched the laws of hot stars adream with creamy pajama eyes

                    and all the hours of evenings & centuries
                    leaving their shell

a last-minute future unfolded its wings
too suddenly beautiful   as the mouth of a bird

                    the white & sweet of it caught in the trap
                                      of its skin

the sky lay there
I tried to pick it up   hoping I too could be carried away

Musidiscorda

                                                            when we bury our
                              dead
                              cities of the future

                              are visited
                              upon us
                                                            like absinthe drawing
a line in the space after your name

funerals
climb up the street falling down   like an old man
                                                            who has lost his hat

candles dance on lonely furrowed brows   the depth of whose eyes
I
can
cut
out

          wind is orange

the air resonates with flies
like rain   like having a wounded animal
                                                              t a l k
                                                         through my head

          the day explodes
          tearing up
              the ocean
                 almed
               in earth
                    clouds roll into madrigals

I imagine they are sails
and you far away at sea

                                                            bending the air
                                                    into avenues of foghorns
                                                    bobbing

before v
        e
          r
            t
              i
                c
                  a
                    l lights   serenely oblivious
                                                      and tooting a tune

                    I watch the moon squat
                    straddling the river
                    of green wood

                    empeopled streets
                    go madly
                    running their mouths
                    in fear of lovers
                    who have memorized
                    their screams

                    I am as I am young
                    among the many-headed
                    pigeons
                    a purple crow
                    hurling itself
                    through busted
                    concrete

120

my funeral is like an old wife
who has lost her cabbage

I want to trace the sound
of your smile
like a conjunction
buried in the palm
my hand

The Blue Distances

                                  dear death

murderer of doves

how sore you must feel   about your
stolen being

               how you
remind me

of a sane inebriate man   sitting at the bar

hoping

he   like you   might disappear inside this quarter-hour

                                          a little waltz of brandy
that dips its tail into the sea

the breeze that makes him shiver

                                        it is all he can think of

                                              clear
in august light

his heart squeezed to a lump   keeps itself warm

                                    flames against a green sky
push out from the holes
of his eyes

the plumed sound of his voice   islanding the earth

                                                        such love
                                    as sings its hands in the air

a birdhouse of junked arias

                            of immense tulips   to fall asleep on or into

                                    the pieces of us

                        going up
                                    slowly

For the Love of Orange

                                                   in my room of red
and brown
curtains tinctured   by a sky that can barely float

there is a little brown language   shot full of holes

and a thin blue light
whose heart   has its tail in its mouth

           for a fix on what air
                             & delicious with creature

as by the simple waving of a wand
rain cuts an exit
        in
      the wall   the places I am now

                  hours
                  into the already marvelous athletics   of distance

                         where blood flows rose of azure
where nerve & bone combinations
are a transparent music
                  answering the deep calls of mother

                 here I lay me down my head to stream
below
the circle of horizon   among the many-headed pigeons
              tumbling
              lovely
              &
              drunk

under the lake of the ocean

I can taste the sound of wind   rising from its well of mud
                                                                    & stars

                                                  its geometry is a warm science
touching my mind
like the weather of a slow kiss

                                        this dream is similar to the future
moving as it does
as the size of a bruise   its sheerest surface blinks
                                                              bending the air
                                                  into a silver-shaped tear
into a numinous & miserable green
banged out
            against the wreck   of an untouched hard core

I feel a love-hallucinated
                    sea
              pulsing
              mad
        beneath the streets

                          the squat of skyscrapers slipping into the earth
                                                        in muffled
                                                      groans
the light opening up the sidewalk
is
wearing
an infinite
      rose
    purple
  wet

                                                   how the sky is inlaid

                  with a discreet opulence
                       & I mixing it
                         with mine   from down here

and then and now all the time
I am returned

undreamed
& seduced by a peace   and move powerfully through silence

                                   as I search for the flower
                    of your lips

               where the gloam
      of cities
& centuries end   and begin again a thousand times

like a picture hung from a wall

like losing someone   and not knowing what

                       the house
                is how
                I
                left it

     the sun turning into itself   is a glistening
                                 rock
                                 in which an orchid   burns

I plan to take a gradual
walk   where the blood comes through it

Praeludium

in all my fire of human becoming
I wear the lovely weather
of shibboleths
on my forehead

I feel the earth breathe
still   warm
trees
bearded in winter

the spruce dreams of the palm

the sage dreams of soft peach

the tree of unspeakable life
waves a nest of thorns
in its arms

I rest my head
meadowed in sleep
on the slope
of a burning rock

every amulet has a sex

the winged emerald is my woman's body

her gentle green tears are shadowed
in my blood

as I write into her
I lie there
like the other room
running my fingers
though rivers of blue hair
a kiss reclining nude
in orange wind

under april moons
a fine rain
anoints my canary
machinery

I eat the fruits promised to autumn

I am speaking from the heart

you have it in the holes of your eyes

songs trickle your name setting off   residua
for the thousand cities
interred in my soul   discorda

desiderata illumines suicided stares   rhomboid
in the boudoir mirror

                                                       caterwaul

outrances swim in the dampness
of my brain   laughsick

in silver weather I fly
powerfully through silence
full sail

clipsing handsome jewels
in my beak
trailing blue vapors

always on infinite shelving
of ledges   the words
get whited out
as like make me tired
as not

Trial and Eros

I'm a refugee in my own
storybook flesh
seeking asylum

—Izzy Oneiric

Ordinary Tones

truth did not come into the world naked
it came   wearing
               a bullet proof vest
opening cans   slicing bread
uncorking bottles
               putting pots
on the stove   talking
in ordinary tones
         sinking   its teeth
into a field of soft peach
            a would be lover
"and you are…"
at the mercy of chance
          carving her initials
into the shadow of a tall tree
two minutes
        of unimpeachable joy
the swirl of your hands
in smooth dirt
          the flash of high noon
a chariot drawn by floating geometries
stepping down
into the eyes of lovers   lunatics
           winking at skyscrapers
at spiral staircases
           drinking up clouds
milky transparent
shards
      of cool thoughts
myopic crepuscular
         tumbler shift
changing rum to champagne
           a sacred spring
lily-shaped   deep purple

a splendid crimson
        the price of death
in ordinary tones

In Lieu of Flowers

in lieu of flowers
balconies
exhale
the sway
of women's hips

I harvest
myself
home
wandering
on my hands   with my head on my feet

blue menstrual seas
shift
beneath
the streets

I garden my shadow with purple light
welding
with poems
my shield
&
on it

o
O
New Orleans
you are wonderfully
poet

intensely self-absorbed
like a late morning
brandy
struck
dumb
by the rain as it falls

                                        on my
                                      cigarette

whose dream is this anyway?

Paul Chasse says the UNIVERSE was created from
tiny particles of dust in Saint John the Baptist Parish

I've been awake too long
and I feel like I'm being
born again
I feel like a fever divorced
from lust
a she-wolf exploding
over your grave
a moan of enormous
revolution
pregnant with a cataclysm
of sounds infernal
& uncreated

                        o
                        O
                              earth
accept this body which
was taken
out of your body
this concrete jangle
of swamprock
this love-emptied arabesque
hemorrhaging
flesh bells
over Jackson Square

              the sunset climbs down
into a triple moon   streetlamps
splinter into worlds
plunge deep
into the holes of my eyes

I am an umbilical cord roped off
& tethered
to the volcano of approval

     even the birds
stop singing and look at me
& wink
at close intervals how do you
feel?
do you feel?

as I kiss the ground
oracular rainbows sprout
from the top of my
shaggy head toward an invisible
sublunary mushroom

  this poem is walking barefoot
as a sign of piety
over a broken glass slipper

Three Poems Past Midnight

the sky is a blue ceramic pot
gone to pieces
        a ship at sea swims
smilingly in my head
plots a course   a nervous magic
from my gut
these lines   an orange clock
the pink of five
tulips at 5pm   the faint dog bark
of afternoon

but really   I've no intention
never do anything
until the moon   wheels sideways
lands on its hands
        then on its feet
stretches out lazy
across the hood of my car
athletic   marvelous
instant calculation
     is always madness traveling
through the world
at this hour
three poems past midnight
        unveiling a pair
of fat thighs
under the horsehair blanket
as night falls to her knees
        letting her red hair
stream into streams   into light
and blood
a thump from your heart
     made of mud and feeling
a sigh
a song from your friends

the palm of your hand   your trail
on the sand
shone in her fur   walked heavily
in her furry coat

Ecce Signum

the moon darts out
      from under a frozen tree
pulls up a chair   toward 3am
looks me square
         in the face
I wipe the sweat
      from bad dreams
off her brow
into a cloud   on a silver tray

       a song trickles in my ear
begs to be sung
I pluck violets   forged from steel
         rods in my belly
the melody begins
        slag from the furnace
a soft cavernous weight
      works its weight back up
I sing to the company
of stars   squatting on my head

how say the people
      the dead the dying
the soon to die
the ones who will die later
         slaves to fate
chance   kings and desperate
men

      I see the sea merges
from a doorway follows
and falls behind

                    our heads strung
together
along the fine thread of sleep
                    along the lemons
of dawn
                    long trumpet blasts
from an untouched hard core

                    over the bull's horns
I trickle your name

Easter in New Orleans

today is feast day

red daises bloom in the ripe womb
of earthquakes

saints press turnips to their lips & kiss
marble shrines

I do not hail from a city of angels
and I am never going back

I sit at the river's edge
like the mind of a shark

scraps of words float by
like tumorous catfish

rain-splotted clouds pound ordinary sweet
canticles outside the Saint Louis Cathedral

all christs hang in museums behind
a curtain or beneath thick plate glass

such is the loneliness here / a strand of pearls
without the pearls / the love and ache of this
old indian portage / this mudlump of town

I feel the river grind her watery teeth on shadows
of skyscrapers / on shadows of lovers idling by

and they go / and days go by / and I feel tired
and sleep lazy / waking / 40 winks & a mule
missing you / it's no help / but it's a good thing

a carton-full of psychedelic eggs
bursts in my mind

I glow numinous alone
listen to the whomp of ship horns
along the river
listen to a tune that lights up
america 1955
curl up under tomorrow's headlines
wash it down on whitebread
or rye

I am lulling myself to sleep now
I am thinking of taking you to meet
my island friends

I stretch out on an obscene sofa / watch the walls
clutch & claw / watch as shadows are crucified & die

headstrong men & women lay buried
beneath an untouched hard core
stick out from the mud of their graves
mouths agape / stilled
frozen / pale corpses
hoping to retrieve the thoughts
they never told each other

you are the poem that lights up
America tonite

Trial and Eros

in giving birth to myself
I learn to fuck & be torn apart

my breasts are like twin goats moved
to death by the morning milk

I am guided by my woman's body
her silver-shaped tears
the sleep of infants
innocent and full of urine

suddenly she is smiling
sniping from the gutters
lilting like angels' trumpets dream
in a charming corselet
made of poems

my thoughts stumble on after her

you are as physical as a disease
I can taste you
the nude distending
inside my head
my crazy bird pointing skyward
dropping down over the pyramids

I am an after hours eternal history
putting this bed to dream
between martinis

each panoramic second clinks
like fresh flowers beneath
your embroidered skin

in the gold of shadows my eyes
are brimming like a chalice

I spill your miracles
under a rock
which is where I lay your heart
to rest

◆ ◆ ◆

I can hardly remember the future
the air of water
the tough magic of clouds
settling into the earth
the piano keys floating up
to greet us

are you happy, sad, not happy?

I
see
ships
lounge
by

and where are you?

I'm here
on the levee
kidnapped
by the 10 years

since I've
seen you

my cigarette is always lit

the cold uneven music presses
my face into wet glass

I'm waiting for you to love me
like water

glyphs of ochre and goodbyes
trail on the ground

Emergency Kisses

for James Nolan

        of the body
is the earth sound
asleep inside
the odor of violets
given off
by decomposing flesh

        I crack open
a jar of light
withdraw my child hands
from the air and sand
I grew up in

        I am a lighthouse
with a neighborly porch
a living jewel box
of saffron
and silk   an inane hero and
his double

what a svelte dream this is

a woman removes her head
replaces it with a chandelier
I pin a Rose of Sharon to my lips
trace my eyes circling the lost
ermines of two caresses

            three blocks down
two floors up

        in "un galope
de claridad nocturna"
I shove the moon off
on a ship

          devour the earth
with an iron spoon

          hitch-hike gray clouds
punctuated by blood
take off down the street
toward Montreal

               I clean the dirt
from underneath my fingernails

pack my bags

     load up the car

          moonless shadows
join hands and dance
incognito
around the tree of unspeakable
life

          the wind is holding
its drum mother

under the influence of autumn
when leaves are blowing
my insides are like purple heather
gnashing my teeth on purple heather

The Red Earth

I was born from a gentle rise
in the left trouser-leg
of my father

my mother's kiss formed me into a fish

inside their volcano of approval
I discovered a legendary
moonsplit plum where I slept
and eternal history
of nine months
in the land of trembling water

the great earthquake of my mother's body
was my first poem

The $18 Martini

the first martini felt cold and very clean

the second martini made me feel civilized

the third martini lived in a country where everything
seemed a very funny joke if I understood it properly

the fourth martini came in looking fresh and
lovely and had a lovely neck and shoulders
and sat on the stool next to mine

the fifth martini took her hair down and drank hot red wine
with spices and lemon in it and smiled at me and touched
me with her foot under the bar

the sixth martini had no honor and no shame and placed
her arms around me and kissed both of my shut eyes

the seventh martini asked questions to which there were no answers
and disappeared with the women inside a mirror behind the bar

the eight martini took the enamel off my
teeth and left it on the roof of my mouth

the ninth martini made plumes of smoke in the air
and numbed the edge of my brain

– there is no record of the tenth martini –

the eleventh martini was a game, like chess, in which
I realized perfectly that nothing should be lost

the twelfth martini wrote a poem:

do not avoid death
play under it

afterlife leaves honey
on your tongue

the thirteenth martini did not say anything
but was just as affectionate

it had a pink rose tattoo on each finger and drew
its forefinger across my throat

the fourteenth martini was hot and dry
and their were flies in the room

the fifteenth martini left behind a note which read
your blood coagulates beautifully

the sixteenth martini sat on the floor in a patch
of sunlight coming through an open window
and washed away the sins of the world

the seventeenth martini had no religion
and drew a line in the space after that word

the last martini was tired

it did not seem a martini at all

I miss the feeling of being held by your clothes

Shrine of Dawn

I was put to the torch
              at the edge of the desert
and placed in a sack
in Jackson Square
                  where honest folk
take to drink
              mayhem & joy
give me my future
for five bucks
              the right to meet
fate with a firm grin
the right to draw
              with my hands in the air
the way I'd like to die

my morning arrives
              on an east wind
a puple breast serenade
pigeons land at my feet
                stare at my shoes
hungry bird gypsies
minus the sky
             O shrine of dawn
tender roseate weave   riff
of corn-ripe
              telephone poles
pink orange gods
dipped in fire
              falls from your lips
looks in   on lovers
lay awake
            silent

the quick morning funk
of bad dreams
                    the shadow of an iron bed

                    I surge forth
down Decatur Street
slip past   what was once Kagan's
explore possible worlds

                    a new transmission
lunch with Laura
a three-headed dragon-tailed dog
                    half man half horse
half hungry
the need for sleep   a jelly donut

                    where I outta be
the Friendly Sea

                    at high tide
a throng of crude ships
                    sets sail on my belly
for dandelions
asters
                    goldenrod

Night Music

while I sleep in the holes of my eyes
fear keeps me awake

I see two rocks clacking
inside my skull

     a bouquet of cinnabar red
and jade
sick and coagulated
crawls
from my mouth

          thrust of maw

strum
of weak amber

     haloed machinations

twisted zounds

s a c k e d

quivering to the beat
of this thud

        I try to withdraw
the hook of my head
and put
in its place
a wooden-peg leg

◆　◆　◆

       as I open my eyes
I depart raging
on my
oblong streel
hemorrhaging spurts
of inky fluid

junked arias

plumes of snakes

spasms of mysterium tremendum

rise up

from the imagination of hell

       I see the sky replaced
by the face of someone
I know

       stars crouch
like jaguars caught
between
my fingers

       eternity stretches
my pocketwatch down
to my ankles
and through the floor

I must dissolve so that I can love you

◆ ◆ ◆

the flavor of blood unto mother

assembles in my heart
        swims across the tips
of my breasts
unfurls
on my thighs

        buxom seeds
trickle through my veins

    on my lip my heart is
a cuckoo for god
flapping
inside the tongue

      on my tongue sits
a winged emerald
flapping inside a conch shell
like a jackhammer
of postmortem fear

I sigh like sweet olives

     sparkle
   and
   burn

and this
my spangled heart
is how I learn
to die

A Voluptuous Sun

                    I waken in golden
and blazing daydreams
nursed on seeds
shorn from trodden wombs

                    inlays of fleshbells
silhouette fiery butterfly
puzzles
over peacock-colored walls

my lover's sigh tendrils my face

                    you are naked   nubile
embryonic   oceanic
veiled
and unguent   an eternal diurnal
clawing its way
out of a blue single rose vase

loams of amorous wet
            snap open
                    a voluptuous sun

                    I see the warm
        waking dusk
lulling shadows to sleep

                    I
            feel
        the moon
                    at my feet

I am a firm fish swimming inside
     your belly
a crocus making its way through
     the mud
the last swan boat to sail across
     the sky

     the sun sinking to reach you
has the mood of this hour

Emergency Kisses II

                    of the mind
is the ocean deep
inside
the parasol of marvelous
prostitutes

                    against my lips
I feel the sigh
of a seismic hourglass

I grind my limestone tongue
into gold coins
                    on the ledge
of your windowsill

          I am a muddy Mint Julep
blossoming
from a discarded gas cap
the prow of the sun
                    spiraling down
into a blue menstrual sea

          it is the 5th of august
it is the time of petulance
and Agamemnon
it is the very hour when gypsy women
                    snatch the air of water
from snowflakes in June

this is when you must minotaur
your cave
this is when you must charm
the devil's sow

charge the temple mount
sacrifice the sixteen starry reptiles
gift their green loins into thin
soft hands

I see blue eyelids on the sun
thorns of rain sliding down your face
trembling delusions
become emergency kisses

I surrender you to the infinite
Polaroid light

If Ever There Were One

o
O future
how much a moment means
back in the day
I'm about the way I feel
        feeling my skin snap back
into words
on a trellis of air

if only you were here
or I there

shadows holding their breath
to strike the keys

        the immemorial wind

a prelude to how everything
can be said

        on days as these
I kick open my grave
skip elegantly out
        nostalgic seas scatter
into blue rectangles
rainbows
blow my eyelashes toward heaven

the distance you will go
have gone

Smoke-rings

he held the saddest the dreariest of flowers
in his hand   love
                        love
I loved someone. someone loved me.
lilac it was exactly that
lilac   lilac
the main thing was that it be pretty
that it give pleasure
all that was dead in his head
in her head
this thin little filthy flower
smoke-rings
they sang smoke-rings at the top of their voice
at the top of their voice

Reincarnated Backward Time

in another time
which is not mine
      and you are asleep

      and having bad dreams

I will let myself into the house
                  on your head

            take a look around

mention something like

   "you have a nice house by the way"
because you do

            I will search my pockets
for three rocks
place one rock in each room

            each rock is made
of moving parts
            which I have made

            the first rock is perfectly formed
egg-shaped
            the size of an olive

you can detect
the miniature image
                  of yourself

      set off inside a metallic surface

            scattered

with white specks
            and small etchings

        the second rock has tight edges
gives the appearance of being
    part of a larger rock

nearly transparent
prismatic
                the size of your hand

    the third is wedge-shaped
an ordinary smooth black

                without question
the oldest of the three

                a slight detail
shows the imprint of a lock
of hair flowing
inward
from front to back

            the first morning
after I am gone
you will hear walking
aborigines
in the pipes of your legs

a song will tear through your limbs

        a song from rocks
made of moving parts
            which you have made

you will carry buildings and streets
                            with you
            wherever you go

      instant cities
centuries

     boulevards courtyards

      common features
           thighs lips
      a swash of blood

     a scene in your life
smashed with a hammer
       seven stories high

    names will lose their faces

gather into a sparrow's nest
       in your hand

     draw you down
in thick cool grass

bury your hands into a clod of clay

an empty tomb will stick to your bones
sweeping and final

you will decide to take a bath
     but go to the movies instead

it's a beautiful movie

you can only laugh

    but it makes you cry

Saying Goodbye to the 20th Century

                In alleys back o' town where Emily
is a state of mind

                    where the vanilla light
is a truck piled high
with broken television sets rumbling through it

men huddle about
transistor radios, listening
                          "people
                          of
                          the
                          planet
poet Dennis Formento
                    has asked kindly

that you join the 20th century
while we're still in it…"

police draw blood sausage from their holsters
counting down .45 .38 .22

antipoem guns reel into place

                                o
                            O America
darling sepulchral garden of Leda
you are a feast
inside my velvet head

                      a funeral
fat with an apple in your mouth
setting out
home to my house / for supper

                         every time I think of you
I begin to urine
before god

an echo of lead melts
                    into a sublunary mushroom

                    I close my eyes
swing my snowy hat
and seizure
transient spheres
to manage this cocoon

                    flotillas of raging
butterfly worlds
hang out of my mouth

          scowl
down
the
page

abbreviate
me
this:

adios, muthafucker

A Bath of Flowers

I wrote my first poem in brown gravy, my best friend was a green candle, Orleans... New Orleans... the bend in the river cleaves to the sky...

—Bob Kaufman

I

The Fuchsine Of The Vine

The View from St. Peter Street

delusions don't happen by themselves. they need people.
consider the sidewalk. the immense solitude of the cracks.
its geometry breathes like my belief in religion. like tapping
a needle to the skin, or a scab, where a fix can find a more
permanent vein. sometimes it's no more than an accident.
sometimes it's both. right now I'm neither. but I'm getting
tired of telling myself that there's some kind of reverse
magic to it all.

The Sky Grows a Hand

Thoreau himself reportedly decided before kindergarten
he wouldn't go to heaven because he couldn't take along
his lemonade shed. this squared the question: the city of
sleepy angels had lemons of dreamless hands, and a finger
for each ring, but was it art? like so many fickle gods the
sun felt its face on the snow. there was no bad weather.
there were only different kinds of good weather. Henry
was four yrs old that day & shook his hammer at the sky.

Shaking the Kaleidoscope
for Megan

I never noticed the moon in the window until you started
living here. I thought it was a bad joke. something I'd look
at if I felt like getting punched in the face after I'd died. now
there's one in every window. one for each color: green, red,
orange, yellow, purple and blue. I snag a piece off each one,
pull it through the window, place it on the floor, move them
around, all the combinations, the best ones. then I take the
colors, the ones that get left out, and squeeze them into that
shiny gold kaleidoscope I gave you when we first met. so you
can put your eye up to it. so you can see what I've always
dreamed I knew. that some mermaids live in trees. that some
unicorns lay their horns at your feet so they don't get cold.
that some angels rest their wings by your head each night
because tomorrow's a long day. o this house is bliss. a holy
of holies. just look at all those goddamn moons. half moons.
new moons. quarter moons. full moons. moons in between
moons. for chrissakes, it's fucking beautiful.

The Little Girl King
for Mina

starting from the hollows of your mama's belly, you arrived
with the birthmark of woman, strawberry hair & long toes.
your name is a gift from one of our favorite poets. one who
wore strange earrings, designed mysterious lampshades, and
whose eyes stared out at blinking earth and filled the page.
this morning you're taking breaths between gulps, smacking
at fingers, puttering bubbles down your chin. I sit my little girl
king on a knee and watch, o green of tulip stems gone out to
sea, pink fishes are beautiful drying on her eyelashes, and like
anything I've done that doesn't make sense, it still does!

The Halo Factory

for Andrei Codrescu

often I mistake the opening in my soul for a knife
which is a curse for the insane. it usually follows
after every polite sentence and unbuttons the blood
on my hip. it was given to me by the barefooted
goddess of dice in the space of a kiss whose smile
tastes like whatever desires you most. there is no
escape. being amused will haunt you forever, as
am I, from having survived this wasted body, and
for having loved more than I could.

Junked at Sea

some dreams are like old galleons that get junked at sea.
this one has a patch with a bad eye and the smell of wet
blood on its lapel. I need a positive economy, an ample
spread of bread, an endless supply of iced red wine, a fat
bird & a village girl. one who laughs like the Jolly Roger
that flies over my head. swords running out of scabbards
stopped into flesh and a trunk of gold. but that was New
Orleans before she became the busted miracle she is now.
most mornings I'm lucky if I wake up feeling like the fly
that got eaten by the plant. today I feel like a short order
cook who can't even get the bacon right. it's a problem that
never solves itself until afternoon. that's when I get back
to thinking I've finally located the lotus portion of my brain.
a trip to the river usually does the trick. there you can marvel
at just the right chunk of concrete with graffiti love scrawled
all over it, and a cozy lizard keeping itself warm.

L'Elephant
for Daniel Finnigan

this is the ear of an elephant. I hold it close to my own
to hear what all the other elephants are saying. mostly
they say they're tired. that they'd like a little peace and
quiet. one elephant doesn't say much at all. he doesn't
have to. he has wrecking ball eyes. the kind that dream
of flattening cities the size of Harrah's Casino, Walmart
and Home Depot. the kind that get all crazy stampede
like after 3am when he's out looking for his long lost
land of buttercups. it's a brutal language.

Tangerines
for Megan

we're on the steps near the river at the Moonwalk. I'm watching
sunlight bounce off ships in a flickering sort of way. you point
out a little girl down by the water popping balloons and add,
"Is that a syringe?" her name is Samantha. she's six years old.
the last time she came to New Orleans, she says, was in her mama's
belly. I gently remove the syringe from her hand. she has a smile
that smells like tangerines.

Rota Fortunae

I didn't begin this pilgrimage without accident. from the
start the shock & terror my parents had made, made me
a case of mistaken natural selection. I was a box seat to
one of life's most embarrassing shows. mine was a million
minds played backwards, a dancing cartoon prison, a defect
of the head that infects all Mad Hatters. but who can ever
guess the weather? this is the subtropics. hurricane season.
some days come down sideways. others feel like a gale of
coconuts. I'm only good at what happens when I know the
ending. when I'm blissfully one sentiment too many passed
longing. and the hours whiz by like this city begins every
afternoon—with an aperitif, and a red wine hat, and blue
I move toward evening, a bath of flowers, and your hand,
which I take for a heart, deliciously garden purplish, just
as I expected, out of thin air.

The Eucharist Tongue
for Anselm Hollo

its meat pokes out slightly from the mouth, then slowly
disappears back to its pew. mine wags from side to side
under the direction of Valhalla and believes in everything
until someone makes it a soup. your mother is my mother.
a little crispy on the outside, pink in the middle, medium
well over an open spit. the flavor is hungry and keeps
the village warm.

The Private Zoo

this story has a certainty like supper. if you're going to sleep-in through the rain, ask the fingers that feed you for long arms. dogs have no human response to weeds that grow out of your head and don't fall off. their point is to swallow. or how one might imagine a conversation like *A Clockwork Orange* without the violins.

The Revolving Air
for Robert Creeley

gravediggers apportion their labors to greet me, a vast
supply of holy water whose eight pints turn to wine in my
veins, a ghost in splendid flower, the fuchsine of the vine
bending into fatal position, wrapping around the moon.
this was nothing a blue sky could do, and filth & pigeons
to climb my way home.

The Story-faced Girl

then there was the bed. then there was the luminous
& butterfly blue painted walls. then there was the upside
down horseshoe and scores of orange light to warm &
stuff my head with beautiful birds. slowly your moving
silently appeared standing in the doorway enough to
explain "sleep is like water, a space that you encompass"
divided by underwear, and the smile hiding your tongue.

II

The Garden Of Lilith

Summer and All

for Bill Berkson

I was a bathing suit in the American idiom, sitting after
a table, eating my favorite flavor—baked banana, honey
& whipped cream. I wanted to make something special.
this is South Louisiana. a four hour exit from Texas.
four lazy blocks from big muddy hulking ships out to
sea. I came to live here as a child. it, too, was late July.
now shiny ABC's have disappeared into my head like
the rings of a tree.

My Little Pin Up Girl, 1943

fresh from mooring the dirigible he called his fingers
to breakfast, Betty Grable's million $ legs, and plundered
the soft gams. could any Joe say no? this was stitched
cotton. some britches go openly. others unbutton quietly
down, like after choir practice, farm-tanned, a warm glass
of Guernsey cream, and glamorous like Tinseltown.

Bird Training

nervous types scare easily. others have accidents over
which they have no control. the hat my head wears does
so, so the birds won't fly out. so I don't terrorize towns
like the one in that Hitchcock film where the gas station
blows up. please write to the address on your scream.

Saint Paul of Bywater
for Paul Chasse

build yourself a paper airplane. wander the universe with it.
you'll need a month's supply of water, an anti space-pigeon
killing device, sun block spf 348 or better, and a makeshift
raft built of Jim Beam bottles for easy travel to the planet
surfaces. and remember when you arrive at that star system
that looks just like ours, it ain't gonna be one of those ordinary
cosmic parallel fuckem-upems. it's gonna be a real doozy. so
pack a lunch and get my ass out of there.

Thinking in Miniature

this is a poem about potting soil. one of those sunsets
that looks like the stuff that comes out of a genie's lamp
after you make it shine. I feel like a spiny caterpillar on
a playground and it's beautiful inside. some of the tiniest
maps begin with a low whisper on the edge of a dark wood.

The Edge of Wetness
for Bernadette Mayer

between your holes & mine, no honey drips like infants smile.
though for a moment, my sureless head dozes songs grown
beneath the sun like a thick oak. then slowly goes back to work
where the maps keep changing, a pair of lips like rose & clover.
two blue moons meet talking in small blue explosions. questions
answered in crimson melt into place. oh dreydl, dreydl, dreydl,
I made it out of clay.

The Magic Self

in the magic self it seems everything has meaning. but it's not long before the chronic of logic & time disproves this theory. today there's no disaster. just lovers vomiting blank stares that drop the temperature in the room. making good nasty love signals the end of this mood. afterwards, we get back into our clothes, go buy some paint, punk and studded with jewels.

Moon Rockets

the work the body does to look good forever is outmatched
by its determination to be a repository for hazardous waste.
it's an experiment of beauty as lovely as a corpse rotting in
a cracked tomb. as eternal as the gook-filled sacks left behind
by cosmetic surgeons. songs whose lips get swallowed by
earth where the plastic-to-bone ratio strains the cosmic scale.
o earth, blessed mama of these sad creatures, Timothy Leary's
moon rockets were not wrong. blast my ashes into space.

The Peyote Coyote
for Joel Dailey

dear Ponce de Leon, as far as the vitamins, we've grown
the plants, breathy flowers, all the positions of smoking
sex—booted negligees, green, purple, plastic and white.
but I can't decide where the eyes should go—the garden
of Lilith's howdy nipples, Cinderella's never castle, the
tawny frogmouth at the San Antonio zoo? will you live
to be 102 too? today I was greeted by bamboo chair legs
that looked just like Aldous Huxley. so I removed my head
and offered it to my guests as a rotisserie chicken. why?
what can be done with faith, can be done without faith,
beginningless from birth, Dr. Doom, or under a glass case,
god temporarily removed.

The Obligatory Kowtow
for Ali Taylor Duplantis

I sat out the reclusive part of my life in a sudden café.
the decision had extreme and fatal results. my ambition
was to be completely forgiven. to be feasted by worlds
that might soon end. to leave their complications behind
just as I had found them—on a plain wooden bookshelf.
there I discovered my one weakness, which was sometimes
my only strength. I had unruly tactics. a language buried
fang deep with its paw-prints in the snow. my mistakes
continued to grow. this has been documented on a piece
of yellow paper. one that has a child's drawing on it (red).
but like my many friends in life, I have been true.

Digging for Earth

taking short strides through scumly watered daffodils,
watermelon weeds, little old ladies lose track of things,
spare livers, interlocking lovers, anything that doesn't
have an expiration date. I'm finally getting all used up.
each morning the smelling salts work less and less. the
house keeps filling up with water. pigeons are nesting
under the bathtub. the raccoons haven't returned. the
clean air act is eating my lunch thermos. the earth doesn't
have to kill us. it's the same thing as loving something.
why bother?

Day's End
for Richard Collins

drawn against sunlight, the murmur of water is a kind
of talk that happens between my mind and a tree. under
the spell of hot afternoon, my body performs a single
monolithic stare to the west. at day's end I swallow
a spectral flower to study the moon and its glow.

The Etherist

originally from a family of hook-headed pirates, the etherist
is probably happy. violent hills of clouds make his fingers
weep softly at dusk. this is also true of busted church
bells & a good nap. if you ever meet him, whisper with
all tender rage your one great calm, then glance amorously
over his shoulder, and he'll remain faceless for a time.

The Snow Poems

When man wanted to imitate walking,
he invented the wheel, which does not
resemble a leg.

—Guillaume Apollinaire

August Days

clamp ink-shaped morning to your forehead
roll it around on your tongue
and go for long walks
in January air
where proper hungry wolves
are pawing their noses in the snow

Home is in the Feet

for Daniel Finnigan

I'm in one of my Dauphine Street moods
sidewalk walking
thru cities
where pigeons live
rolled up like pajamas
worker's hammers smack 2x4s into place
9am light tricks the mind
into a slow cigarette
it's nice to be a balcony with green eyes
explosion on the lips
trinket wonders
snipe from the gutters
elegant and rough depending on what
the occasion demands
today is the early spring
of early winter
I am addressing you to you
home is in the feet
staring out of a photo-machine forever

In the Meat the Snow

give me your slow blood
the color of broken doves
my faith lay in those lips
whose lies smell of heaven
you who go on being born
despite geometry
god & the cruel motion
of stars aimed
at this thin dime of earth
in the meat the snow
is father to a madness that never sleeps
a loveliness like a thousand miles
of bad road
we descend like sad butterflies
over the wet places
waiting for the perfume temperature of genius
drop by drop
in torched light
our pretty wings leave dark stains
muscled on floors of infinite sleep
there the world lives alone
in a roomful of busted music
boxes that bump into each other
shod & crowned with sick flowers
the sound signs itself into a noose
gulping tears
ancestor ratios
how the mouths we kiss
drink from our own sweet skulls
the thoughts we never told each other
placented bursts of prayer
scissor the horizon with
cutouts of thunderfold

The Weather of Heaven

the heart you are
wearing its little fur hat
sweeps out the odors
of love from rooms
tougher than flesh
and I am more often
never anywhere
but close to home

In Winter

I love my animal heart
my blooded heart
longing has nothing to do with it
people of the world took me
for their own
when they smiled & called me friend
I offered them a silver-shaped tear
when they offered me love
that was not love
I led them to the golden dustheap
counted my litter
and ate them one by one
laugh if you can sleep if you must
I used their hands for antlers
and glued them to the weather
inside my head

The Infinite Disorder of Prayers

under high superstitious ceilings
sleep is a frightful rock
a dungeon of paradise
where I find my old self
waiting for me
the head floats by the ankles
I feel the bare room
trembling yellow in its labors
busted souls traveling
through the world at this hour
get recycled
and a little less desperate
like the difference between god
and bad information
I wish everything slender of flower
I wish gray light turning green
on dazzling snows

Crime & Breakfast

morning is a strange city
we visit it in mirrors
room to room
banging cigarettes around
like crime & breakfast
are the two great joys in life
the head gets turned on
one staggers quickly
between moves
somehow the excitement
only seems to last
so long as there is the risk
of affection

The Sleep of Dusk
for Gina Ferrara

sometimes years I am circused
by delicate children
playground sounds
the head swirls smooth dirt
laughter stills the brevity
of yellow
umbrella rain
holds the eyes in braids
measure it in your ear
hear the mood of the trees
sewn from the button
of your child heart
bounce the sound
off the highest cloudtops
all secret knowledge is built
like a fallen roof
where the birds fly in
I costume the air
by the heavens of these worlds
each telephone pole sundown
brings a quiet music
windswept silence
dreams of a crooked fence
my body is the sleep of dusk
smiling age nine

Terra Incognita

the law of chance is against prophecy
believe in your brain
laughter crackles like hell-fire
to kill a roach for example
with godlike indifference
or that loaves of sunken fishes
are both sad
& spectacular at age 20
but I'm 32 now
and love affairs are cruel
they fill the hours with inferior christs
dark aspirations
& blow the mind into a dazzling void
later remembering this
I'll go plenty mad

Smiling Over the Waves

smiling over the waves
I saw god hanging up the telephone
laughing adios
in a pale fuzzy coat
his face was a flower
stuffed with snow
I decided to take a bath
but went to the movies instead
& all the bathtub
hair in the world couldn't
save us from drowning

La Dia Monde

in Venusian feral wonderment
we spread our legs
through mirrors
where our holes make meals
of each other
the geometry is simple
& ancient
ice floes form the fingertips
of one tiny thousand dreams
a stillness blossoms in the eyes
waking up orange mounds
of sighs
any tendency toward symmetry
guides the secret interior
to its fiery heaven
where the scent of hours
drifts endlessly to a point
of perfect rest

Buzzard Luck

I hardly ever think of May 3, 1967
when mama's hips squeezed into a scream
and I came moaning my head out her belly
in the hallway of Baylor Hospital
she thought she had a tumor in her leg
her doctor said she had a tumor
but not in her leg
we spent our first winter in Dallas
then sold the house
and all the snow with it
today it's New Orleans and August
where rain is faster than snow

The Farewell Machine

listening to Pearl Bailey while
lying in bed
I realize I don't need
to see a shrink
break up with my lover
or go underground for any hard
adjustments to my already
busted soul interior
I breathe through a head
of exploded lightbulbs
madjuggler potionists
stir my insides
to a luminous boil
when night's reddening
furnace fades
my hands will form an invisible
bird gesture
and slip slowly
toward the circle of horizon
lovely to be born
and here to have seen it

Where Late the Sweet

the juice knife has its cut arm
and the eventual sex of its death
so too how we have loved
slaved on this tendency
toward forever
from both ends I practice
looking out through the top
of my head
the aperture of a felt hat
makes pictures of your moods
hair hung black to the floor
unfolds into roads
swollen or sad
with the amnesia of being
I picnic my hammock of heaven
in the garden sun
praising avocados & chickens
I am too tired for sleep
and the wet funerals
that rake mud over our heads
and soup our bones into a cold roux
I am more blue than violet
a little weather that traces the bodies
of water I would sail over
if I tripped from New Orleans
to the Atlantic Ocean
brief hands form the mouth & face
and drag the moon
by its feet
beyond any miracle of lies
when all the lights go out in cities
this funeral is from the eyes down

Bride in Cold Tears

often I find myself being swizzled
by silent revolts
mad dwarves live in the pink
forest of my clothes
because of this
people look at me with great sadness
but not on their account
I think of my favorite color
all of them
like the days themselves
moments like certain flowers
bloom empty in the hand
if the instincts are right
the sweetest meat
should be around the claws

Thinking in Utero

I dance the seven days
live lump turquoise weather
ambrosia the snow
trick rope suicides
turn tears into a neck of grief
you have your four hands
in the melt of reach
a vast island sea-filled moon
I sail through concussion sleep
pawning angelic notions
for a future cigarette
loyalty to anything or anyone
except a faithful anonymous
performance
is hard to maintain
O expert kisses I wish you
were more here
the air is singing to be born
on a stolen landscape
all my eyes see
blue possible sound
the beard of a god whose hand
strikes blue possible sound
now or even

Dream Hands

for Jonathan Kline

if you have a piece of silver rocket hose
either by means of a map
or with a needle in it
you can walk right out of the scene
into the warm blue velvet
part of your life
light up a cigarette
peel yourself into an orange
and symphony an entire
language of snow

Subzero Globs of Light

odd by the calm of an empty room
I stare dim religious
out the window with eyes
bigger than a houseplant
while serious godfeet
tramp New Orleans into a watery
oblivion
everything is working
toward the rear of my heart
I'm counting prayers instead of sheep
subzero globs of light
are inches from my eyeballs
it's more than a lack of sophistication
some of them are coming at me
wicked like details
in Bruegel's *Les Patineurs*
the southern sky is full
of asking delicate questions
some nights I can take the weather
other nights I'm more afraid
of people than I am of roaches
they talk differently
it's a beautiful first class headache
one of these days
I'll figure out how to work
the giant wings that lay folded
in my hands

The Page of the Fortunate Monkey

life moves on
sometimes without us
take green for instance
my equally naked heart
full of risks and no speech
I always want to know
where the trouble can come from
the gloom inherent
in spiny truths
it was nothing I had to do
the door was secretly open

Any Blue Movie

for Jamey Jones

dear friends—the snowflakes
of Armageddon are us
it's a blue movie
dripping baffled
& disconnected like the tomb
of christ
and as with any twilight
blasted with milk
we held it just enough
to hold it
until the clockwork jewels
broke off
then it was anyone's
trial with Judas

The Wilderness of Things

I think I know the trees
Will never love me and we're here as accidentally

—Bernadette Mayer

In the Blunt Opening Space

in the blunt opening space
the threadwork holding together the castle
prepares a meal for you and the children
tonite the silk flowers on the table
presume too much
king of this kitchen
a fat frog with a crooked crown
pulls up a chair to his plate
thoughts neatly stacked in his skull
"embrace" is the wrong word
to ring the bell of the dharma
or that I pride myself in believing
this book is made in love for love

L'Amour qui Attend

inside the miracles of sleep
drawing sunlight
from every direction
there is one instance I am
at a love to explain
whose gift of person
is ever beyond compare
fluttering in the open sky
so crowded with birds
that templed garden
the cypress the juniper
the sandalwood the cedar
calling your name

Through the looking Glass

through the looking glass
which I pass
I'm only tall enough
to lie down
as you remain
a kept secret
but to speak as though
you were the inventor of love
or to gaze at peonies
had I been wed to one
a more preternaturally
desiccated rose
I could not explain

At the Necropolis

firing his red arrows at the necropolis
the dead don't move much
thus Cupid improved his aim
first at night then later all day
he emptied his quiver
then took his darts to the backcountry
whereafter 10 winters and 10,000 arrows
his mind grew & grew
until one morning a clucking sound was heard
but the only egg to be found
was earth-shaped
and as Cupid looked out in all directions
he saw what Little Red Hen hath made

The Ides of August

this is the tropic of fish
a shoal of oystered pearls
to teach me nothing is love
but a momentary lapse of wave
dropping away until the next
pushes flotsam of jellies & seaweed
a little higher onshore
back home the air stretches out
thick white blossoms of crepe myrtle
as if I've been in a coma
for nearly two years
I just wanted to wake up not screaming
and to return to this waking life and you

A Lover Who Calls

a lover who calls
is the ideal dinner question
lounging in a comfy chair
whether the weather
changes the scenery
to the tune of red shoes
or the air of a silent movie
I plan to do both
en masque
O prickly coitus
O little peach of emerald hue
trussed with furry purple cuffs
dancing to Clair de Lune

The Plum Peach

one difference between watching
the paint dry and the grass grow
is a plum peach
ripening in the sun
brushed out from the eyelids
an oil-sheened hand
of alabaster & rosehips
circling the slope of breast
scent of snapdragons & mums
mouthfuls of warm erection
a smooth palate of wine spilling from the vine
and with the pleasure of thoroughness
until the throng of bed arches still

Philosophiae Naturalis Destructus

most dreams that block out the sun
after I wake up
are a useless combination
of devout romance
and unwanted third party love affairs
eventually the spell wears off
as I catch the logic of light
warming its feathers on a wire
while the rest of me
considers Isaac Newton's equation
force = mass x acceleration
up the street under the wheels
listening to the boxcars go by

Friday the Thirteenth

flashlights in the surf
morning frogs in the parking lot
scattering like birds
it's Friday the Thirteenth
in the Florida panhandle
and everything's happening under my nose
as I look out at the waves
the beach leaves an extraordinarily
walked-in impression on the eyes
worst case scenario—Mina and Blaise
bury daddy up to his ears in sand
and from where I sit
the world is unanimously ocean

The Afternoon in My Head

for Mina

the afternoon in my head
is a slow passing train
sure-footed ducks
waddle from the lagoon
for clumps of bread
the pigeons the nutria arrive on cue
today's list also includes
a bag of boiled crawfish & blue crabs
at the newly repainted playground
though my favorite surprise
to keep the mind occupied
is on the backside of city park
below a sign that reads "pony rides"

The Who That Is I

the who that is I
enters through a doorway
so hardly noticed
posed opposite
the other life you dream of
a form of pause stops the light
from reaching my brain
is it just mere appetite
that loses its flourish
I take the poison
I take it down
this is no spectral flower
to feel cuckold and numb

The Apartment Garden

tonite I wrap my heart in shiny tinfoil
and present it to you
as I would any other meal
how much living
have we done
caught between a throw rug
and a pillow on the floor
and but for the youthful asparagus
or mushroom hats I adore
I've yet to avoid the head-on glare
of passing suns
together we are the perfect match
mongrel pure & faire

The Hand Is a Word

the hand is a word
everything comes to it
like a tightrope
lit up with beautiful creatures
tiptoeing to bed
so as not to stir
the sleeping little ones
thighs poised quivering
ever nearer an instant
in the shape of yes
while the muted fireworks
light up the balcony window
brilliant enough for any of the Graces

Dream of the Lotus
for Jim Cass

were I a hushed jump rope of sound
I'd swear the galaxy
was an inch across
pressed between the pages of this book
here's a leafskin with tunable eyes
this one for the gift of water
brining up at the bottom of a bottomless pond
this one for the dormant seed
sprouting from the muck
in an array of hot pink blossoms
this one for the wish to become
any creature of your choosing
rivering between the two-skies of your mind

Ten Thousand Suns
for Blaise

moving sounds
stretch out under my feet
ten thousand suns
crawl up from the ocean
they wear their hats
like pretty wooden bowls
but where is the "wow" in everything
that's Blaise's favorite word
to describe any deservéd phenomena
I can only guess at what he sees
somewhere between 18mos & 40yrs
we're both here
shoes of elfskin & flip-flop toes

A Denby for Your Thoughts

eating bad flowers the math is always wrong
the voice tends to break
its timbre spills over into its intonation
what someone says
ends up in your arms
at the precise angle which light crawls toward shade
it was this kind of afternoon I became
the secrets I aspire to be
piti à piti zozo fait son nid[14]
a bel canto orchestrium of tongues
a Denby for your thoughts
breathless with adoration
the calla lily the oleander the foxglove

---

14 *piti à piti zozo fait son nid*; Creole Proverb, Louisiana; English translation: *little by little the bird builds its nest.*

Above the Roofline

how rarely one may love
where others have failed
I keep my notions in bed
pierced by a glance
as elegant or rough
as the occasion demands
it's a mathematical formula
to turn up the thermometer and sigh
let's open the bedroom window
let's ride off in a canoe
above the roofline
as the moon shrinks even higher
never unpleasant but effervescing for miles

Behind the Ailanthus

from the Ice Age to Mickey Mouse
there's no apology for the human soul
I dream for all the animals of creation
slithering back to their nests
flowerets of lady's slipper & tiger lily
fill up the yard
where a blue candle burns
O you whoever you are
behind the ailanthus
and whose absence has slept at my side
like a silence nothing interrupts
I am the look on the face of a man
whose only regret is the setting sun

The Oort Cloud[15]

a square halo is an awkward fit
for a diamond-shaped head
so is finding my way
back to heaven
never having been there
my father wasn't very good at that
I'm hoping it's not genetic
my urge to fly
comes from a place
just beyond the orbit of Pluto
that's where burning rocks
hurtle themselves toward earth
at life-stopping speed

---

15 The Oort cloud is an immense spherical cloud surrounding the planetary system and extending approximately three light years, about thirty trillion kilometers from the Sun. This vast distance is considered the edge of the Sun's orb of physical, gravitational, or dynamical influence. Within the cloud, comets are weakly bound to the sun, as well as passing stars and other forces, and can readily change their orbits, sending them into the inner solar system. The Oort cloud is the source of long-period comets that were pulled into shorter period orbits by the planets. Two recent Oort cloud comets were Hyakutake and Hale-Bopp. In 1950, the Dutch astronomer Jan H. Oort inferred the existence of the Oort cloud from the physical evidence of long-period comets entering the planetary system.

Summer Is Ending

summer is ending
brightly through a window
with the moon above my head
steadily you smile
like "yesterday" means last Friday
or earlier today
I'm preparing a dish of bay scallops & wild rice
it's a nice place to land
on the living room sofa
slight thighs bent at the waist
Mrs. of Everything that's mine
with all our former selves
magically entwined

She Walks In Beauty [16]

she walks in beauty
barefoot Kubla Khan
La Belle Dame sans Merci
pushing a Red Wheelbarrow upstairs
"Om" is the key word
two shoulders bent for a kiss
where Fire Is Born
which no flood puts out
Long Night Moon crooning
over wet magnolias
a faint stirring remains
or disappears how long ago
O Lakonian river so greatly loved

16 The title "She Walks in Beauty" is taken from a poem of the same title by Lord Byron; "La Belle Dame sans Merci" is the title of a poem by John Keats; "Red Wheelbarrow" is taken from William Carlos Williams poem titled "The Red Wheelbarrow"; "Fire Is Born" is the name of a Mayan cultural emissary born in the city of Teotihuacán c. 450 a.d. during the rule of Spearthrower Owl; "Long Night Moon" is the title of a poem by Megan Burns; *Lakonian* refers to an ancient region located in S Peloponnesus, Greece, land of the Pelasgians in pre-Hellenic times.

Gender-wise I'm Ambidextrous

gender-wise I'm ambidextrous
as I prefer love to anything else
but more than that
I want to draw delicate
& incomprehensible pictures
with my crayons
all over your mind
where sounds compress the vowels
into "flesh peach" "canary" and "robin's egg blue"
though unlike those creatures
chirping quietly to each other
behind the wires of their cage
my nature is not so easy to tame

The Headless Torso

behind the dark door of secret earth
the headless torso
is a skeleton of form
baring its lips
and what a woman
a dream unto herself
combed in perfect locks
rising from the bed
as if uncoiled from a vase
I can even feel the snowy pelts of December
blown in by gusty winds
and across the path which lay between us
the sturdy wooden bridge that brought me here

The Wilderness of Things

except that we were
alone in a Mexican hotel
a round room of air
quietly undressed
each buttonhole
wearing an au naturel grin
one tat for the Japanese expression of "love"
the second of a nude girl straddling the moon
the third a coyote's forgetful dream
swallowing whole the heart of another
whose whispered countings
became *my* walking song
in the wilderness of things

A Pot of Lips

This world is simply the curtain
concealing the true mise-en-scène
of the eternal spectacle

—Jean Arp

Waiting for the President of Argentina
in collaboration with Daniel Finnigan

I.

Never believe presidents on their birthdays or
                on anyone else's birthday for that matter

                                                        the pride
                                                            &
                                                        status
                                        of their luggage boys[17]
                        must NOT be compromised

                "Do you suppose Mr. Argentina's wife
                                wears a crotchless bodysuit
                                                on trips to the States?"

other questions such as these
                                may never be answered
                —but we must try—
for the sake of Van 302
                and for water towers climbed[18]   we must try

                                        STOP
                        you are now entering a restricted area[19]

                                UP ABOVE
                the view from the cockpit
                        says it all
                                the tarmac with its glorious white dashes
                                the immaculate gold
                                        wings on the captain's chest
                                                could he pass a random pissing contest
                                                if his President demanded one?

---

17 Our mission.

18 (See Finnigan, childhood daredevil).

19 Area 51 of Louis Armstrong International Airport.

                    the voice from the tower
                  rolled through his head
                like a fat joint on a hot Argentine afternoon

          this was no ordinary landing
                there would be
                          - possible graveyard death spirals[20]
                          - bomb sniffing mutts
                          - sexy consulate babes on the make

                and try we will

II.

          Ah, oh, nea yea thus
          bring me yonder wenches thither
          their behinds treat me like dinners
                    fit for the Sultan of Yemen
                          the head corn husker
                          the President
                          of El Presidente

Articles itemized for transport:

   2,040 percussion rifles
   30,600 lbs of soap, musk, gold
   8 deluxe tanning beds
   a quantity of peas & biscuits
   571 crunchy taco shells
   27 pairs of padded acid reflux sleepwear
   a set of utensils for the King (which cannot be itemized separately)
   4,372 cubits of abstract bravado[21]

---

20 (See John F. Kennedy, Jr.).
21 (See Maradonna, World Cup Soccer Star).

and brave we were
that day
the day of the President

Always know nothing when receiving
a King
they like you better
that way   there might be treats in it for ya
and balloons if it is time
for dinner

never get help on your way
get it first—then go
The President will respect you
The President might take
your advice on
- ties
- tires
- fishin' holes
- bitches

A little higher up on the scale
furious cravings for Big Macs, vanilla milkshakes
& fries are replaced by the face of someone
we don't know

III.

Tanning is a process
like airport patrollers with pipes of Sherlockian Wonderment
but remember that we are
the processors
as like make me dinner as not

Alas, the idea of presence, Mister Patagonia
himself, his hallucinated likeness, urgent repetitions
of secret safety passcodes, it is our duty, we
must find camels, organize, then

cut it open from hoof to hump
drink the gracious hearts of passers-by
& shake hands as though the President

    were already here
      because getting water is serious-faced business
       we must confer with the authorities

"Do you speaka Spanish, un porquito? Okay, you take
orders only from these two men, that other man, and
the person in charge of the belt carriers. You will know
him when you see him. He has long hair, and is mostly
shaggy in appearance."[22]

       one step back for Van 302
       one step forward for Mr. Argentina
       one step below a bell captain
       two steps above the orange cones
       of direction
       and omnificence

   la perra likes mesa
     they smell good—give them treats
  and Christopher Walken
    becomes a continent unto yourself

the president would rather
    have his people push a chevy
      than drive a ford
    but this is luggage
    what's he got,
      diamonds on the tip?

---

22 Fabulous behind the scenes Secret Service drivel.

IV.

Strange how the trees
    on the other side of the runway
        remind me of home

      though I don't feel at home here

          whose voyage is this sword for ten men?[23]
no one knows
    but lo, it is a handsome day
      & we're waiting for the President of Argentina

Although we are waiting like we've never
    waited before, this day, like any other day
      reminds me of any other day—and that,
        my friend, is gorgeous
        and for health
          the President's daughter
        stirs me
        and stands like Sex
          I see beautiful women
        all over my
          days and future

What is the reason for our waiting here, again
    like all the others times we have, breaking
      our own hearts over President's daughters
      and being hungry?

          I'm hungry too!

---

23 Sailor talk from *The Golden Voyage of Sinbad.*

Epilogue. In late July 1999, Argentine President Carlos Menem, along with members of his cabinet and the Minister of Defense, visited New Orleans. Shortly after his arrival, the President requested that his entourage be chauffeured to Gulfport-Biloxi, Mississippi for a gambling trip. I was chosen to drive the vehicle which transported President Menem's medications, formal attire, as well as his mistress' evening gowns (his wife didn't make the trip) to the Doubletree Hotel in downtown New Orleans. Daniel Finnigan drove another vehicle which transported antique percussion rifles, argentine china, silver flatware, etc. In November of the same year, the New York Times *reported that President Menem had been ousted on charges of embezzlement stating that Menem's flamboyant lifestyle had drained the coiffures of the Argentine National Treasury.*

Ode to Cannabis Insanitas

in collaboration with Thaddeus Conti   *for Bill Lavender*

Untrammeled as we are
in our self-service matrimonial attire
bestride ALLA cum louder & JEHOVAH the chauvinist
and besieged
by the JUSTICE of No Peace
more silly-stringed news dribbles from the east
while a silhouette of recompense
dirges for the moon's absence

No less, my boot soles are abscessed
with waiflike pustules, which, when divinated
with counterfeited T A X insignias,
and other holographic tragedies
found en route to lesser museums
scream WE THE PEOPLE "Hallelujah!"
"Get those soldier boys out of Fallujah!"

Launch The Thousand-Ships-In-A-Bottle
containing the Corpus of the Cremated
American Constitution

Set a course for an All Inclusive Reality
blanched in the sun of Childhood Memory

Give us growth spurts of supernaturality
such that the spaceship containing our brains
delivers us closer to that indomitable realm
of poet goliaths which gave spawn to B I L L
                                                A
Lest We Forget that same primordial goo   V
from which he rose also brought forth   E
                                                N
melting ice caps, dead kennedys, and the diminishing D
populations of african savannahs   E
                                                R

O William "Two Snakes Fucking" Lavender
whose birthrite puts the mojo back in our mojitos
which we worship and glorify
'tis right to give you praise
for someday soon all the oil of this world
will be sucked up
and The Earth shall begin anew
without humans to *fuck it up*
whose poems
were The Terrible & Beautiful Song of their demise

Slingshot of the Golden Loam

in collaboration with Andrei Codrescu

Dear Mister Saucy Pants (aka. God)

you shine like honey
                and bed your lust
between us & the blood
of a thousand hungry sleep scrolls

where's your manners?

You let them fundamentaliss
  and comuniss
run your business for You
  when Your children here we are
    in our midnight milkmen suits
      do your work kaleidoscope-like &
        animated by so much love it hurts

        give us back our do-nothing prayers
               Your twisted sons

or a knife or a bottle or a club or a gun

just knowing You are hurtling
        somewhere on this dark night
        explodes
bad comedies in my head

around the bend I see astrophysicists
    leaving the convention hall to murder You
      with particle accelerators

We give you political asylum, Lord
    and honey to rub on your ontological weariness
      and a bell to summon us when You are frightened

We come running innocent blobs of blood & faith
too broken by years & thoughts You never told us
We live a ruin on busted street corners

shoving songs
            in Your children's mouths
where laughter seems out of place
and the intention
            of the organism is to scream

            but that coup de foudre look on their faces

is a wolf to our sheep
    we shed the fleece & go on eating the grass, nubby skulls

on hillsides, gypsies on beds of cana
            ready to march this mother father land

laid end to end
quilt of lovebites crosshatched by scars
            we are the freckle hunters parachuted
            behind the enemy lines
                of the bean counters

            we drag our parachutes in front of us
                through doors
opening
into misplaced paradises
                    the head hangs
the hands
                    handcuffed to bedposts
            where sleep is perfect
and more terrible than air

EFFUNDAM DE SPIRITU MEO SUPER OMNEM CARNEM

The Kingdom of Expulsion

in collaboration with Andrei Codrescu

Always in fisted steel city air
I'm in the weather
Launching tiny pinballs
On the lake of the ocean
Your mother is my mother
Whose fever glows blue & slightly wet
And her galoshes squeak in Russia
In 1918 and in New York in 1965
With a whole ocean in them & she
Fills them with seditious moustaches
86 proof whiskey & Tibetan prayer-wheels
How dying to is like this: Midnight
Encounters spilling up thru swamprock
Daniel & I dumping the clutch in Jackson Square
The radio singing lidded Billie Holiday eyes
And I feel like pulling a shiv from my boot
& screaming something incomprehensible
Some sort of reverse miracle
That would transform the St. Louis Cathedral
Into a giant masturbating pelican
So the birds can reclaim their kingdom of expulsion
O wonders of wonder, I want to break the mind
Of this place into an orgy of woolen babushkas
Sounds leave the tongue like the secret
Interiors of broken zippers

The Good Shepherdess of Nether
in collaboration with Andrei Codrescu

when hurricane names reach
    the Greek alphabet
it takes us a long way away from the theory
    of original sin
and the common housefly

    all the way to the common sin
of wishing it was not the way it is
and the original fly
  did you ever see one this blue, Dave?

    no but I've heard whispers
from the blue depths of the wounded Omega
whose mouths are zero-shaped
    and whose songs are all in the key of blue

    as you at your bluest
      or you over there at your pinkest
we are situated where the alphabet forms
  in the mouth of Monsieur Dada Styx

    near the headwaters of the 17st Street Canal
it's Monday, August 29, 2005

O Good Shepherdess of Nether
    throw me a rope made of your best linens
pull me up to your thighs

Bark of the Pelasgians

in collaboration with Ed Sanders

I live in the mouth of the sleepwalker
  whose song hails from The Drip-Drip
   Constellation of The Pelasgian Sea

I am also the scribbler of The Painted-
  Bark Book whose tell-all scriptorium
   is the story of The Upsidedown Tree

The *Bhagavad Gita* features a Huge Tall Tree
ancient and sacred
with its roots up to heaven
and its leavèd branches
spreading across Wide-Breasted Gaia

Illuminating the Pelasgians
those ancient dwellers from where?
from Other Dimensions?
or from brains a-growing from roaming
on the edges of melting glaciers

I draw the Final Glyphs
upon the Painted Bark
to quell the Violence

The Dog Is Dead Asleep[24]
in collaboration with Simon Pettet

how great is sleep, the gentle and the wise
alas that I should be
so old, and you so small
I, who never kissed your head

so small, so wrinkled, so gentle, undulating
but rising to a point
how great is that
how great is sleep

uncertain labor at best
to formulate what is best—
what eyes to stay, what calm hands
what musculature, what breathings

now forbidden to climb the garden stair
and take a leak among the onions
leeks and garish orchids
or brush away a tear

---

24 This collaboration was inspired by lines from Ted Berrigan's copy of Yvor Winters'
Collected Poems.

Some Valleys of Landscape and Measure[25]

in collaboration with Peter Gizzi

it doesn't mean fairy dust
or dumbfuck stories
        of creation and apocalypse
        in Sunday school
Percival was hungry for a story of his own

there was a green unapproachable
sound in his ear
        the blue of Ophelia's portrait
        a blue picture of love he might draw
while wearing his long hero's cape

it's like saying grace after every meal
and feeling the sound
        leave your lips flapping
        toward little equations
like the word *hummingbird*

but I'm already past mid-heaven now
bouncing light off the clouds
        in skiffs and shafts
        I feel like a museum
of miniature things—sow bug marches,

water striders, willow spear, trilliums
hooded owl, Macchu Picchu
        Hawthorne, widdershin
        gimbal lamp, swivel chair
ma mère, harbor flares, punkdom
even the clapboard's chipped paint

---

25 This collaboration was inspired by lines from Peter Gizzi's book *Some Values of Landscape and Weather*.

working to rise
from the deep trajectory
          of anything half-forgotten

I want April to sleep in the privileged
          nostalgia of a toy boat
          free of its moorings
the incremental journeys so spoken
          scribbling warm milk
on rugs, the geese overhead, "Closer,"
they call, "closer."
          the wheel, the wagon, the way

now that's a life — sonorous echoes
          tattooed to a shining event
          were it not
for the bastard child of Sir Galahad
          waving, walking
          into the Percy grass
somewhere between beetle and boojum
everything that's needed from me to you

Glomming the Crwth[26]

in collaboration with Anselm Hollo

dear hombre in the treetop hat

    hello

    & how it goes

    & should a dog read this at

some time in the future — c'est si bon

        to hocus the animals of pursuers

            twinkling upon these oaken shelves

as the goddess stands

    in front of her cave

    blood on the saddle!

    tumbleweed to dream in

what goes where, here

        now to say (in zomboid)

            wee terrible human, a love supreme

---

26 This collaboration was inspired by lines from Anselm Hollo's book *Man in the Treetop Hat.*

Too Far From New Orleans (Mexicali Blues)[27]
in collaboration with Paul Chasse

outside the guitar
and the mad maracas
                compete with taxi poems
          diesel fumes
a whuff of the Gulag
      permeates the cabana
              inside — beam & semen flow
      "I don't care if it's a woman, a boy or a donkey"
a hole is just a hole
and that's what matters, baby
               and on his red silk pillow
sits Cupid preparing his knives — cheap red
dresses, soft white shoes
            12 hardons for a dollar
        mota, chiva
& tamales sharing mouths
Montezuma dances snakes from a hole in his vein
hers, yours, any mouth wrap your tongue around it
and lay the cornerstone
this steamy swamp
too far from New Orleans
              belching Mexicali
blues

---

27 This collaboration was written in Exchange Alley in the French Quarter.

Rose Stigmata (The Motion Picture)[28]

in collaboration with Paul Chasse

dear Big Muddy of the most high mighty shitsnake
believe you me, three hundred thousand years of steel
plying your angry waters
your hush quiet
& I, on the tugboat, seeking your liquid heart
am amazed by the silence of your thunder
the oily blackness of your light
I'm hard pressed to find reason to dally elsewhere
like mother tankers whose silver smokestack lungs
sing rocks belched out of skies over Slaughterhouse Point
"but when the skeetas bite your face, they're hungry"
and now for cooler climes, the old point bar
Gibson-axe-horn-head-fix-jesus-motherfuckers
and fat weaves
just a beer a a shot baby, then we'll go home
the wind velocity of our table is too strong for navigation
like them burlap bell ride bone keys flying grim sirens
fuck the mosquitoes, full speed ahead! whiskey dreams
and funky days here on the turtle's back
oh Big Muddy, your mama done me good
put rice in my belly
okra through my toes
from here on I swear I know everything bout Egypt-o-logy
it's am three thirty, just one more shot & a beer
then we'll go home baby
I promise

---

28 This collaboration was written at the Old Point Bar in Old Algiers.

Mr. & Mrs. Houdini's Treacherous Voyage[29]

in collaboration with Bernadette Mayer

changing white wine to red wine
    shit-be-gone gift wrap
        that unworried-look on your face
    when I said "no brakes!"
sorghum cooking frog(s)
    man-eating skunks
        inchworm Xings
    Lucky-Bo-Diddly balcony seats
Humming Turtle Room dreamcasts
    beer-swapping foot massages on Algiers' ferry
        dastardly thunderstorm candlelit porch-a-thons
    giant puppet show Virgin Mary sightings
Cha Cha Malgooni's (sic) lifetime achievement award
    resuscitation of peonies with hazmat suit [Daniel]
        donut volcano appreciation hour [Amy]
    jedi mind tricks on police [Max]
many-headed pigeon vision quest [Sophia]
    strawberry rhubarb pie concierge [Marie]
        taoist egg collector & flamingo safari [Zack]
    Evil Knieval stunt double [Hector]
auditory hallucinations speaking backward in Yodanese [Ted]
    earthworks & igloo sweat lodgings [Atticus]
        backyard dessert eating bear competition [Grace]
    pork death pot [Phil]
Pot Pot Pot & The Lighthouse Philharmonic [John]
    high priestess of cephalopod [Sor Juana]
        one of three evils [Harris]
    mythical beast witness protection program [Michael]
plymouth rock tosser & distinguished chair sitter [Simon]

---

29 This poem is a compilation of various shenanigans instigated by Bernadette Mayer, myself, our friends and family during our visits together in East Nassau, NY and in New Orleans.

global poetry warmer [Brenda]
Arthurian round tableists [Peter & Liz]
Apple Dumpling Gang leader [Tom]
deep water rescue team [Pierre, Nicole & Miles]
flying lessons with Underwater Goosebill [Jamey]
Ed Teach & Mary Read [Tony & Lee Ann]
whatdya think the weather's like in Buenas Aires? [Anonymous]

The Treehouse Aquarium Cathedral Room[30]

in collaboration with Bernadette Mayer   *for Grace Murphy*

alack if you push the nipple button
even algebra, loaf bread, shiny boats
of cantaloupe, rice to be counted
baby pine cones, busted church bells
higher than our knees

alas if you press the vagina telltale
russian trigonometry, emmenthaler breast bread, luminous piroques
of honeydew, blackberries to be transmogrified
infantile locust nuts, broken synagogue glockenspiels
more lofty than our ears

the morning seemed practical when I woke up
obsessing you (flagrante delicto)
memorizing its caress, our walking
through august's no rain &
the auguries of known conversationalists

the night became rude when I gained consciousness
overwhelming you with claustrophobia (ad astra per aspera)
visualizing its bear hug, our perambulating
through bar harbor no snow &
the precognitive natures of people who talk too much

let's have fun at everything
cotillion balls, ancestral compost
strobe-o-phobia, menu pounding spoons
it's such easy feet and more in the world
than shipwrecked bath toes

---

30 This poem takes its title from a room of the same name in Grace Murphy's house
in Woodstock, NY.

284

let's go to the Columbia County Fair
coq au vin fish balls, descendants' fertilizer
fear of lava lamps, a lovely text hitting the afterlife
it's hard for elbows and bears, they're more
like wildlife than any onion blossom

yet from crab nebula to the ox
honeysuckle has saved us
the trouble of brain and hard labor
snuff out those torches, drink blinking lights
disappear into your favorite color, a huge tadpole

yet from the mourning dove opacity of the cornea
to the mosquito, spotted touch-me-nots have saved us
the harassment of cerebration and work under duress
kill those fascist faces, ingest stuttering illuminations
evanesce into your chosen hue, an immense baby frog

how I love takes time to know
this ho-hum fucking universe
its all hours, its ostentation
of peacocks, its busyness of ferrets
its parliament of owls, its sloth of bears

where I adore used-up bears when I move over
cette do-dah-day prickly galaxy
its peak internetishness, its showy flowerishness
of mounting doves, its chaos of iguanas
its convention of pheasants, its ménage à trois of beignets

stranger things have happened
and they've all happened to me
in old sleepy houses or on porches
talking with Bernadette and everybody
knows not just where the Tsatsawassa flows

more amazing thises and thats have occurred
and they've all happened to me

in ancient morpheus-ridden teepees or on verandas
conversing with little bear and all
are not cognizant of where the cup of water goes

say more love what your sex
is feeling, your gentle call for
frank language, let's have it
snow now "big with bedspread"
he whom virgins cherry-toppings

articulate further dearest what males
feel, your shy admonition to
direct russian, let's have it
rain now "pregnant with quilting"
he whom the cherries eat strawberry-rhubarb pie
                            with vanilla ice cream

in the utopia I've never seen
sleep is the only index
she wears a kind face
left on the bookcase to dry
I could pause almost anything

in the noplace you've not viewed at all
morpheus is the sole arbitrator
being a she, he dons a generous demeanor
abandoned on the shelf to desiccate
you could stop nearly a train

being with child the picnic forest
is strangely singing eyes, coyote
yoked hosannas, a strong soap after
contact, some needles don't even have
a haystack, "Hello Gretel, I like bread!"

pregnant the al fresco dining woods
is oddly vocalizing things you see with leopard
yodeled alleluias, vehement borax after reaching

the extraterrestrials, many sharp implements don't even
have sheaths, "Ciao God, let me have some poires d'anjou liquor"

in mute groan testimony the sandwich
should always leave the table
a little bit hungry, melt into ice
a mouthful of kiss-fat possum
everything but the goblets

in autistic moan irrelevance the veal cutlet
should always exit the octagonal horizontal thing
a tad ravenous, fracture into crystals, a large serving of love
zaftig mashed potatoes, puréed turnips, cranberry sauce
everything but the turkey itself & the glasses filled with bread

far from any city of angels
lovers slop & feral their glad eyes
heaven came as a weapon
that couldn't touch us
even more than I can't now

a long way from truth or consequences
paramours smudge & beastly their delighted peepers
paradise came as a pineapple
no way could it palpate
nor can I shock you

dear sor juana, you were never
too quarrel, loose curls grew out
of your clothes, bypassed their
bedtime, the right number
of years, fingers & toes

dear brother john, you used not to be
very bicker, immortal tendrils accumulated like tractors
from hip-hop attire, blinked at
our daffodillian canopy chronology, the correct google
of digits, years and appendages, Mr. Margin

we wore our lips in reverse like any villain
in every movie from the waist down stammering
little alphabets, biscuits of wine, I had a million minds
as birds usually do, steamed with pleasant odors
and the secret religion of oyster petting zoos

we bore our brinks backward like bad guys
or bleeding baklava in all b-files from the bare
midriff below just bleating
tiny primitive buttocks, muffins of brain, my mind
was filled with butterflies
as is the bunting's wont, sautéed with tantalizing smells
and the secret insect rebellions of cloud museums
and boy-girl caressing yet prison educational institutions

of the nude masterly iris to hold
dear nothing ever happens
looks up to the sky
its fine methyls, inchoate fist
and no piano to taste home

if the naked mistressly crocus to be tenacious
of adored one still noli me tangere
puff the magic dragon seems to have been elected
its excellent fast-food grease, garbled punching tool
and all lack of stringed instrument to swirl
wherever it is I live, in this case
an underground space off the so-called grid
I might go so far as to call it a cave but
I wouldn't want to supply any clues

upweather safari bends cobalt gong
tuff manners, a slender off-light
yes between sighs, our daily muffins
coming of age, one a peacg
the other an apple with butterfly wings

tripping above atmospheric conditions blue buddhist bell
volcanic etiquette, a skinny subnormal glow
fucking like the sun, our quotidian biscuit-beignet
getting old enough to devour a pomegranate
or a blueberry grenade with monarch airplanes

now that we are all love
hog's head cheese should make us happy
played over loudspeakers, proscenium moon
burns yellow, the river swims by in ships
working gears, shut eyes poured out like stones

maintenant that we are terribly adoring
aspic will render us boring, parlayed into sor juana inez
de la cruz, auditorium-like crescent, flagrant fuchsia
creeks croak over in pirogue-like things laboring shafts
closed optic instruments emanated forth as scarified pavements

from the middle in, my heart is made of lettuce
a nutty hollow between the eyes, a wounded lemon
southerly treadles mense ganja sister of squid
this is an epitaph that reads backwards
and never to memorize the trees very definitely

avant the center hard, my organ of cardiovascular regularness is
                         an arugula of location
a macadamian vacation betwixt the optic organs (sic), a pierced lime
all tessellated and blenny, northern railroad tracks, monthly
                         marijuana, relative of cephalopod
cette sepulchral epigram contains the following ingredients:
                         like a snake or any spider, perhaps a recluse
and no way to learn by rote surely the serendipitous sassafras,
                         ahoy!

The Birthday Wish List

in collaboration with Bernadette Mayer

1965 pink & purple Ford Galaxie convertible
17 doz hypnogogic oysters
clairvoyant lobsters (if you can find them)
half a rib rack of reincarnated Ganesha
1 jar of colossal squid or masterpieces
discount griffins
4 wheels of Versailles cheese
trip for two to any continent that begins & ends with A
7 sacks of mexican jumping beans
pockets filled with chocolate, or deirdres
the unauthorized biography of *Sinbad the Sailor*
subscription to *Animal Dreams* or related publication
a page of titles for poems
a new squirrel
The Sex Life of the Jivaro by Michael Harner
It's Hard to Stop by Bernadette Mayer
So Why Stop? by Dave Brinks
a dress made of peonies

The Prodigical Sun

in collaboration with Geoff Munsterman

this was the case of my laughter
    the tabu, betel palm, liquid lard,
macaw feathers, smoking frog,
    head-hunting, a scalp dance
landward, seaward, seeking the eldest
    tribesmen, a water being, the dead's
nearest of kin with a butterfly mouth

    the bald belly of a trout buttering
its fins in streams cold as logic,
    landlocked, liplock doddering
like milk from mama tarantula tainting
    holy water softens a cauterized
wound, the jayhawk, the bug husk,
    survival willing kisses like a lit wick
conflicting battlegrounds and burial mounds

    for six years the sleeper slept beside
a small round pit dug in the ground.
    in the seventh year, on the morning
of the full sap moon, his hands made
    a circle in the sky calling the clouds
to darken the horizon—chanting *make*
    your roads come forth with living waters,
may your roads reach all the way to dawn,
    let our spirits' feasting-house be ready!
I with my garden darkened foliage, I with my
    leaves and lowana tree tops, I with my
hornbill dwellers, I and every dirty little beetle,
    even the yam kulia, that we may finish
these roads together, all under the same sky!

    and green grew the bedrock dosed
with clovers, each petal each patch each

fitful meadow trembling with moonbeam
widening the circle—worshipped and central.
        one waved his wounds around, the other
showed his sword, but both hoped for the road.
        teeth, claws, and thorns or wound, bruise,
and pool of blood—the water offered shelter
        as grackles cracked their beaks on beads of
rain and praised no one method above others,
        the wood reeds driven in basin sand anticipate
the spirits plucking lush ones up for noise joyful
        as the moth lost in the lighted hinds of fireflies.

Nice Hat Asshole[31]

in collaboration with Thaddeus Conti   *for Bill Lavender*

I was a dark Magellanic cloud
climbing into the backseat of a convertible
the cigarette holes in my shirt
were no Copernican myth
something desperate was trying to re-enter my soul
at a bad angle of descent
what do you think you most resemble?
I am a dull thud
bounced from a moonless landscape
a glass slipper longing for the bride of Frankenstein
and while fewer tragedies have been more true
most nights I can't even remember my name

---

31 This collaboration was written at the Gold Mine Saloon in the French Quarter.

The Caveat Onus: Thirty-Eight Caliber Warning Shot

in collaboration with Richard Collins

the sky of january is not blue
    it's that premonition of a february bruise
and I feel like all my ruling planets
    damned virgins and dame archers all
have turned against me
    their storm surge breasts
so I'm painting myself out of the picture
    still clinging to the frame that holds us
to include anything that doesn't include
    a levee like the great walmart of china
hurting myself or anyone else
    who gets in the way of my morning profite roles
it's like that moment when everything starts
    without a cup of coffee beans
following you around like a baboon of despair
    his kaleidoscope sphincter a peephole of regrets
O Maelstrom of Maelstroms & Abominations
    Bless us Ignatius Repititious
you've transformed the city of new orleans
    as new orleans once transformed us upon a time
into a busted-face emotion no one can explain
    to the beat-up lovelies lingering at the bar
and like the watermelons of st. bernard
    breaching their demon seeds in the night
it's hard trying to pretend the waters never came
    to bless us with destruction

Osmosis Cosmosis[32]

in collaboration with Vincent Farnsworth

the thin blue sun
comes through an open window
                    and my heart with its tail
                        in your mouth
becomes the bird you see
juggling green slices of light
                        in the trees

                    the sun goes down
            the birds create lights of
                        constellation
        from their sleep of
            suspended
animation
coma: I bleed into your map

        an evening gown slips
down into a distraction
                little babies
                        dragged about in red wagons
shedding all the hair
        of their life
                        into the crazy field
            hedgerows of emotion
                        light cracking open
            broken glass on the tongue

        this fever is your fever
            with all its stars asleep at 60mph
                rubbing up
            against my fuzzy cigarette

---

32 This collaboration was written at Orleans Coffee Exchange near Saint Louis Cathedral in the French Quarter.

if the heavens held still
                as the red dot cigarette
     for one evening we could
understand what's wrong
                 with our constant vibration staring
                      finally give the birds
                            their glorious victory

           and us ours with soft purple
minds coiled behind silver eyes
      the afternoon walking lovely
                  through our quiet heads
       on the streets of new orleans
              where pigeons live rolled up
                    like pajamas

Harmonica Virgins[33]

in collaboration with Bill Myers

here we are at the Dragon's Den
in the fried Sears silvertone
wrapped around my mirror with tinsel lilies
and staples flounced and splayed
through body parts sleeping
in the dance floor air
under broken sunglasses
as like smut makes me horny
as crotch swells
with Disney cartoon animals
swollen egos
overconfident Godzillas
loitering in new tennis shoes
the pain of outdoors and mothers
sweeping across my desert
with fugitive Indians and bus lines
through ancient nuclear test sites
I was there fur-lined and wary of everything
we ever knew ourselves to be
and at this point
I guess our friendship ends here
still spilling love
out of Archimedes' jacuzzi

---

33 This collaboration was written during the *Madpoets Express* poetry reading at the Dragon's Den.

Simple Pi[34]
in collaboration with Jonathan Kline

dear the Rosetta Stone of my slave ship,
you have yet to sojourn my truth, you have
yet to fever my tree, the taste of strange fruit
among pine cones of privation, slum lords all!

tonight this country 'tis of thee, o shining sea,
creates an offal for my headsprung backwithal
like flowers, I silent second line, A capital E!
if I were a dog, would I dream of the feathered

thighs of swans, the oak's acorns, the spatula's
meaty patty of beef? o blessed Beouf Gras in my
maw, I was meant to be born in the month of
killing pigs, but was made to wait till the trees

were dead, singing cleavers in the kitchen
a studied glance between skin and metal!
if I wrote the story of each of us, if I transcribed
it in pictographs of my blood, would you

read it then, sieged by nobody but me, swash-
buckling moonshine? That fingernail is the same
in Borneo, orange to yellow, a glowing ember
in white, this forbidden *paradis*, this pearl du mal!

---

34 This collaboration was written at the Homedale Inn.

Dear No God[35]

in collaboration with Bernadette Mayer, Philip Good, Elizabeth Garcia

there we were bumbling kids lipsing
Zuckwheat Bydeco, little fingers, isopropyls
please leave your isopropyls at the door
one more round of gingko
so much color is abound
berries of loudness & light & love
it's so very bright here
I feel good, so good
the stomper is stomping
down the beaters of the beaten
gooey and lo, how say the people
coddling tears lost today we
saw 9 crippled men watching Buckwheat
sounds against the no whatever world
the nowhere everywhere
and our there-ness kept coming through
otherly motherly southerly
cheers y'all, love, the everyone

---

35 This collaboration was written at Molly's at the Market on Decatur Street in the French Quarter.

A Dirty Halo

in collaboration with Jimmy Ross

I'm backstroking under a full moon
trying to find my way out of a dirty
halo, had some seaweed hanging
like she'd just come back
from mermaid school—to the school
of lost and found mermen, ex-boyfriends whose
walking papers said "I snore too much"
several years ago—sodomy
that's a side of me I haven't
rolled over on recently, as long as it's
not Canadian, or the General of the Salvation
Army, hold your hands up
and you can scratch the full moon's chin,
pull his dusty whiskers, or was it that scent
of conquest, the great hill of Rome
Ignoremus, Ignoromulus, such work is dangerous
'tis a wolf's breast you're sucking,
plugging holes, every excuse, every exit,
and still, escalators are like women
with too many corsets tied too tightly
too slightly, the last moon before the frost,
changing our course, please give
god my high regards

INDEX OF TITLES AND FIRST LINES

Titles appear in standard type. First lines appear in italics.

Uruguayan-born French poet Comte de Lautréamont once proclaimed, "Poetry is made by everyone. Not by one!" and Dave Brinks emphatically agrees. Brinks has been a stalwart of the American poetry community for two decades. He follows in the great cultural tradition of many New Orleans visionaries who hail from the Crescent City such as artist George Herriman, poet and film critic Parker Tyler, beat poet Bob Kaufman, Civil Rights worker and poet Tom Dent, and novelist John Kennedy Toole. Brinks also counts among his forbears many others  who have worked and lived in New Orleans, and considered the community as seminal to their artistic visions, including Walt Whitman, Lafcadio Hearn, peace activist Fanny Ventadour, publisher Eugene Jolas, composer Harry Partch, poet Bob "Rainey" Cass, jazz saxophonist and poet Bruce Lippincott, painter James McGarrell, jazz poet ruth weiss, photographer and poet Anne McKeever, sculptor John Scott, publishers Jon Webb and Gypsy Lou Webb, painter Hazel Guggenheim McKinley, and poet Everette Maddox.

As for his own work in the New Orleans community during the 1990s, Brinks co-founded (along with poet Paul Chasse) the legendary Madpoets Express Poetry Series at the Dragon's Den in the French Quarter, and he also co-founded (along with Andrei Codrescu) the New Orleans School for the Imagination. In the next decade, Brinks launched the highly touted literary publishing outfit Trembling Pillow Press as well as 17 Poets! Literary & Performance Series at the Gold Mine Saloon, also located in the French Quarter. At present, Brinks is the publisher of *ENTREPÔT, the Brain Trust News in Arts and Letters;* and also editor-in-chief of *YAWP: a Journal of Poetry & Art.*

Born in 1967, Brinks is a native New Orleanian. His family has lived in the Lower Mississippi River Delta region for many generations. His mother is Acadian French and his father is Choctaw Native American. Today, Brinks works and lives in New Orleans with his wife, poet Megan Burns, along with their three children Mina, Blaise and Issa.

Brinks' poetry and essays have appeared in magazines, newspapers, journals and anthologies throughout the United States, Canada, and overseas including *The Nation, Callaloo, Exquisite Corpse, Xavier Review, Shambhala Sun, Metaphora, Steaua, Vlak, Tingujt e erës, National Geographic Explorer, Louisiana Cultural Vistas* and *Gathering of the Tribes*. Additionally, his works have been featured on National Public Radio's *Hearing Voices* and PBS' *News Hour with Jim Lehrer*.

The Secret Brain, Selected Poems 1995–2012 is Brinks' seventh book of poetry published in the United States, including the critically acclaimed *The Caveat Onus* (Black Widow Press 2009). Brinks is currently working on a biography of early jazz pioneer and clarinetist Emile Barnes, as well a new poetry collection titled *The Geometry of Sound*—an experimental, cross-disciplinary study inspired by the *I Ching*, and centered around a new poetics he refers to as "Dynamism" that explores the origins of alphabets, ideograms and pictographs, with specific focus on linguistic genomes and phoneme-based patterns found naturally occurring in the environment through hexagonal structures and sound frequencies.

In 2013, Brinks' plans include serving as director for the non-profit organization Imagining Communities through the Cultural Arts (ICCA), and also unveiling a new publishing imprint diVerse cultures; as well as reinvigorating the New Orleans Institute for the Imagination—all for the express purpose of establishing constructive, intercultural relationships with communities, nationally and internationally, via innovative projects, publications, workshops, festivals and symposia specifically designed to engage new, interdisciplinary, cross-cultural exchanges among artists, poets, social scientists, educators and cultural visionaries between the New Orleans community and respective communities worldwide.

TITLES FROM BLACK WIDOW PRESS

TRANSLATION SERIES

A Life of Poems, Poems of a Life
by Anna de Noailles. Translated by Norman
R. Shapiro. Introduction by Catherine Perry.

Approximate Man and Other Writings
by Tristan Tzara. Translated and edited by
Mary Ann Caws.

Art Poétique
by Guillevic. Translated by Maureen Smith.

The Big Game by Benjamin Péret.
Translated with an introduction by
Marilyn Kallet.

Capital of Pain
by Paul Eluard. Translated by Mary Ann
Caws, Patricia Terry, and Nancy Kline.

Chanson Dada: Selected Poems
by Tristan Tzara. Translated with an
introduction and essay by Lee Harwood.

*Essential Poems and Writings of
Joyce Mansour: A Bilingual Anthology*
Translated with an introduction by
Serge Gavronsky.

Essential Poems and Prose of Jules Laforgue
Translated and edited by Patricia Terry.

*Essential Poems and Writings of
Robert Desnos: A Bilingual Anthology*
Edited with an introduction and essay by
Mary Ann Caws.

EyeSeas (Les Ziaux) by Raymond Queneau.
Translated with an introduction by Daniela
Hurezanu and Stephen Kessler.

Furor and Mystery & Other Writings
by René Char. Edited and translated by
Mary Ann Caws and Nancy Kline.

The Inventor of Love & Other Writings
by Gherasim Luca. Translated by Julian and
Laura Semilian. Introduction by Andrei
Codrescu. Essay by Petre Răileanu.

La Fontaine's Bawdy by Jean de La Fontaine.
Translated with an introduction by Norman
R. Shapiro.

Last Love Poems of Paul Eluard
Translated with an introduction by
Marilyn Kallet.

Love, Poetry (L'amour la poésie)
by Paul Eluard. Translated with an essay by
Stuart Kendall.

Poems of André Breton: A Bilingual Anthology
Translated with essays by Jean-Pierre Cauvin
and Mary Ann Caws.

Poems of A.O. Barnabooth by Valéry Larbaud.
Translated by Ron Padgett and Bill Zavatsky.

Préversities: A Jacques Prévert Sampler
Translated and edited by Norman R. Shapiro.

The Sea and Other Poems by Guillevic.
Translated by Patricia Terry. Introduction by
Monique Chefdor.

To Speak, to Tell You? Poems by Sabine Sicaud.
Translated by Norman R. Shapiro. Intro-
duction and notes by Odile Ayral-Clause.

forthcoming translations

*Jules Choppin (1830–1914) New Orleans
Poems in Creole and French.* Translated by
Norman R. Shapiro.

Poems of Consummation
by Vicente Aleixandre. Translated by
Stephen Kessler

WWW.BLACKWIDOWPRESS.COM